THE BOOK ON HEALTHCARE IT
VOLUME 2

What you need to know about HIPAA, Hospital IT, and Healthcare Information Technology

JAMES SCOTT

THE BOOK ON HEALTHCARE IT VOLUME 2

Copyright © 2015 James Scott

ALL RIGHTS RESERVED. This book contains material protected under International and Federal Copyright Laws and Treaties. Any unauthorized reprint or use of this material is prohibited. No part of this book may be reproduced or transmitted in any form or by any means, electronic or mechanical, including photocopying, recording, or by any information storage and retrieval system without express written permission from the author/publisher.

ISBN-13: 978-1514331361
ISBN-10: 1514331365

CONTENTS

PREFACE..VII

ETHICAL ISSUES WITH HEALTH INFORMATICS..................1

BRINGING UNIFORMITY TO THE WEB, MOBILE AND
    TELEPHONE CHANNELS FOR HEALTHCARE................9

HEALTH MANAGEMENT INITIATIVES WITH BIG DATA
    AND ANALYTICS CAPABILITY......................................17

MULTIPLE SECURE STRATEGIES THAT SUIT
    HEALTHCARE OPERATIONS..25

POST EHR-ERA IN THE HEALTHCARE INDUSTRY.............33

KNOWLEDGE AND QUALITY OF HEALTHCARE DATA
    AND INFORMATION..41

IDC -10 AND MEANINFUL USE OF ELECTRONIC
    HEALTH RECORDS...49

TOOLS AND STRATEGIES FOR QUALITY
   IMPROVEMENTS IN HEALTHCARE............................57

CLINICAL PRACTICE GUIDELINES FOR
   EVIDENCE BASED MEDICINE..65

CHALLENGES IN MOBILE HEALTH..................................73

PROTECTING AGAINST ANTHEM-LIKE ATTACKS..............81

ANALYTICS AND DATA MINING IN HEALTHCARE..............89

RISK SHARING BETWEEN HOSPITALS AND
   OUTSOURCED SERVICES...95

RISKS INVOLVED WITH UNPROTECTED DIGITAL
   HEALTHCARE DATA..103

UNDERSTANDING INFORMATION SYSTEMS
   ARCHITECTURE..111

THE DIGITAL DILLEMA OF HEALTH INFORMATION
   EXCHANGE..119

THIRD PLATFORM TECHNOLOGIES IN HEALTHCARE.....127

YOUR PATIENT'S HEALTH DATA IN THE CLOUDS...........135

THE PRESSURE ON HOSPITALS TO IMPROVE THE QUALITY OF MEASUREMENT, PAYMENT AND BILLING SYSTEMS..143

PRIVACY AND SECURITY OF HEALTH INFORMATION.....151

PREFACE

The Book on Healthcare IT: What you need to know about Health Informatics, Hospital IT, EHR, HIE and Healthcare Information Technology Volume 2 brings you a complete and up-to-date overview of the key issues related to the adoption and use of information technology, communications and healthcare, with detailed practical information to support students, professionals and other stakeholders in the field of healthcare. Health Informatics, an evolving specialization, strives to improve the quality and safety of patient care.

This book addresses the concepts, tasks and skills that professionals need to achieve the nation's targets for health care, and cover several aspects of healthcare operations, broadly – privacy, security, ethics, new technologies, mHealth, best practices and quality improvement.

You will find detailed discussions about the best practices followed in the healthcare industry towards achieving the goal of better care and "meaningful use." Several strategies for prevention of data breaches are offered as the move towards EHRs and HIEs has opened up additional fields of concern, mainly related to the storage and sharing of digital data with the risk of loss of privacy and security of patient information.

This book discusses ethical issues and ways of mitigating the risks involved concerning outsourcing and sharing information as the healthcare industry is now outsourcing certain services to focus on their core competency and to provide better care to patients.

With Health Informatics, hospitals are rapidly moving towards implementation of newer technologies that support their functions more effectively and efficiently. Read about the use of third platform technologies such as clouds and mobile devices, telephone channels and the Web, along with use of Big Data and Analytics capabilities. All these fields are extremely important individually, and this book effectively discusses how their uniform use helps improve modern health care.

Learn about different architectures used by information systems. Moving forward, this helps in understanding how hospitals are using different tools and strategies for improving the quality of healthcare they offer patients as the industry moves towards the post-EHR era with Evidence Based Medicine.

ABOUT THE AUTHOR

James Scott is a "7 Time Best Selling Author" and lecturer on the topics of Cybersecurity, Informatics and Critical Infrastructure Legislation. Mr. Scott has authored multiple books such as: The Book on Healthcare IT Volume 1, The Book on Healthcare IT Volume 2, The CEO's Manual on Cyber Security, The Book on Mergers and Acquisitions, The CEO Manual 4 Kids among others.

Mr. Scott is a member of several think tanks that study diverse aspects of legislation concepts that effect regional and national economies and corporate communities such as: Aspen Institute, Chatham House: Royal Institute of International Affairs, The American Enterprise Institute, Economic Research Council, American Institute for Economic Research, The Manhattan Institute and The Hudson Institute among others.

ETHICAL ISSUES WITH HEALTH INFORMATICS

Although mechanical aids are being increasingly used for diagnosis, it is difficult to replace the five senses of the doctor when examining a patient. Tests done in a laboratory can never replace careful observations. A diagnostic robot can never replace a good physician.

Ethical questions continue to evolve in social work, psychology, human subjects' research, nursing, medicine and affiliated fields. However, the key issues are generally well known – numerous educational, scholarly and professional contexts have dealt with major questions in bioethics. Although health informatics has been in public view for decades, ethical matters in this field are less familiar. In all the health professions, some of the most essential and engrossing ethical debates are now raging in health informatics.

Contrary to popular belief, confidentiality and privacy of electronically stored PHI or Patient Health Information are not the sole concern of ethical issues in health informatics – although they are of vital importance and significant concern. Apart from the several important legal and regulatory questions that informatics spawns, there are other ethical issues as well, such as –

- Selecting and using appropriate informatics tools in clinical settings

- Determining who should use what tool
- Deciding the role to be played by system evaluation
- Obligations of vendors, maintainers and system developers
- Using computers to track clinical outcomes as guidance to future practice.

Health informatics and its related ethical issues may be explored as a significant intersection among several professions – ethics, applied computing and health care administration and delivery. Such an exploration can safely begin with computer related ethics and bioethics, both very popular fields.

Public health programs are an inter-organizational and multi-professional environment today – with the involvement of health services and several other organizations. It is indeed a challenge when developing IT security measures and information systems necessary to suit this complex context. By sharing information freely in these programs, all involved organizations can be expected to work together towards a common goal – promotion of health care. However, such an ideal scenario is practically impossible to achieve in practice.

One reason could be that the system development process ignores ethical issues. Ethical obstacles arise when sharing the use of geographic health information in public health programs and this affects the design of information systems. Concerns related to confidentiality are generated because of geographically referenced health information, influenced by organizational and professional codes. Disregarding ethical issues, often results in prolonging the development process for public health information systems.

APPROPRIATE USE, USERS AND CONTEXTS IN HEALTH INFORMATICS

Provisions of health services have changed drastically since computers were introduced. Technologies in health professions now build on the prior experience to adopt additional devices, tools and methods. For instance, clinicians often evaluate appropriate evidence, presuppositions, standards and values before performing most health related interventions such as prescription of medicines, genetic testing, surgical and other therapeutic procedures. This development has resulted in emergence of issues related to the protection of PHI, technical research and political debate.

Technological developments have made availability and access of public records very easy. Therefore, information and deductive knowledge about a person is much easier to get at than ever before. Moreover, with different forms of engagement in everyday life today, it is becoming increasingly difficult to withhold personal data. For example, with the structure in health care rapidly shifting to a patient-team relation from the earlier one-on-one patient-physician relationship, the concept of confidentiality is growing increasingly vague because of the several parties involved.

This not only leads to a reduction in the ability to control the use of personal information, it also increases the fear of misuse among the public. Therefore, the public is more concerned about privacy rather than about the accuracy of data and technical constraints. Given this fact, it is surprising that the constructors of regulation and laws and developers of information systems often neglect privacy issues in public health surveillance.

Currently, there is ample evidence to prove that electronic laboratory information systems improve access to clinical data when compared to manual distribution methods, which are mostly paper-based. This leads to an obligation to use computers to store and retrieve clinical data because that improves care with an acceptable reduction in time and expense. However, with the existing clinical expert systems, there is less evidence to suggest that they improve patient care in typical practice settings to the same level.

Compared with simple reminder systems, the intention of clinical expert systems is to provide a more detailed and sophisticated decision support for diagnosis and therapy. Cutting-edge research and development is still underway in maintaining and creating expert systems and related knowledge bases.

In many ways, humans are still superior to electronic systems. In the healthcare arena, compared to electronic systems, humans are –

- Superior in understanding patients and their problems
- Efficient in collecting pertinent data from all phases of clinical practice
- Effective in interpreting and representing
- Excellent in clinical synthesis.

Although humans are currently superior at such tasks, such a claim is subject to periodic empirical testing.

PUBLIC AND TRADITIONAL HEALTH INTERVENTIONS

Public health and the traditional health interventions in clinical settings have much in common. However, there exists a difference in ethics for public health and the ethics followed in traditional medical practice. While public health tries to maximize the public good, traditional ethics rely more on the individual's relationship with physicians and other professionals in health care.

This contradiction leads to a situational dilemma – clinicians are required to balance the interests of an individual against the interests of the public. However, that does not mean that public good alone triumphs while privacy rights of the individual can be ignored.

When health data is shared outside the healthcare organization in inter-organizational contexts, maintaining confidentiality becomes more of a complex network of interactions. However, sharing data should be a natural process, as the organizations usually work together with the common goal of promoting health. Ethical conflicts arise, mostly when sharing health data referenced geographically, in public health programs and this affects the design of information systems.

APPROPRIATE USERS AND STANDARDS OF EDUCATION

As with tools used in other domains, those used in health care such as the informatics systems also need users who are trained, experienced and educated so that the outcome is effective and efficient. Catastrophe is predictable when inadequately prepared users use such sophisticated tools. Health professions have a large and complex domain, with very high stakes. Therefore, user education and training take on moral significance.

Expert decision-support systems provide an insight into the appropriate users of health care related computer applications. Potential users of such systems may include government and insurance evaluators, patients, students of health sciences, paramedic personnel, physician's assistants, nurses and physicians. However, it is difficult to define each of the groups as an appropriate user, unless there is clarity on their intention for using the system – the exact clinical question they expect the system to answer.

The appropriate-use spectrum starts with medical and nursing students employing decision-support systems for educations purposes. This use fields no controversy, since the tools actually convey sufficient quantity and quality of accurate educational content. However, controversy starts when patients, managed-care gatekeepers, patients and administrators use expert decision-support systems for assistance in making diagnoses, in selecting therapies, or in evaluating the appropriateness of the actions taken by health professionals.

Additionally, there can be legal concerns related to negligence and product liability. For example, when patients gain specific counsel from health-related products instead of general clinical advice or when such products are sold directly to patients rather than only to licensed practitioners.

Evaluating the System as an Ethical Peremptory

Moving towards best practices in health informatics should always include ways to measure whether the system performs as intended. Such related measurements pave the way for controlling the quality and obligations for system developers, maintainers, users, administrators and other players.

With a comprehensive evaluation program, a health care organization can implement and optimize an information system ethically. For this, a ten criteria scrutiny of the system is useful:

1. Is the system working as intended or designed?
2. Is it being used as intended?
3. Is it producing the desired results?
4. Is it working better than the procedures it replaced?
5. Is it cost effective?
6. How effectively have individuals been trained to use it?
7. What are the expected long-term consequences on how departments interact?
8. What are the long-term consequences on the delivery of health care?
9. Will the system have an effect on organizational control?
10. How do effects depend on practice setting?

CONCLUSION

People have different reasons to protect their privacy and confidentiality. Most people regard privacy and confidentiality as a right and the protections help to accord them respect. Therefore, people may not feel the necessity to provide any justification for keeping their health data secret. A person may assume that privacy and confidentiality are entitlements they do not need to earn, to argue for or to defend.

A second, more practical reason for protecting privacy and confidentiality is this benefits both – the individual as well as the society. When patients are confident their health data will not be shared inappropriately, they will be more comfortable disclosing their condition with clinicians. A successful physician-patient or nurse-patient relationship depends critically on this trust, helping practitioners to do their jobs.

REFERNCES:

Ethical issues in public health informatics: implications for system design when sharing geographic information
http://www.sciencedirect.com/science/article/pii/S1532046402005270

10 Ethics and Health Informatics: Users, Standards, and Outcomes
http://eknygos.lsmuni.lt/springer/56/379-402.pdf

The Value and Importance of Health Information Privacy
http://www.ncbi.nlm.nih.gov/books/NBK9579/

BRINGING UNIFORMITY TO THE WEB, MOBILE AND TELEPHONE CHANNELS FOR HEALTHCARE

Health service delivery all over the world is poised for a sea change. This is being triggered by the prolific use of mobile devices and wireless technologies in achieving the objectives of mHealth. On one hand, there is an exponential rise in the use of mobile technologies and applications. On the other, there are new opportunities coming up for integrating mobile health into currently existing eHealth services. Moreover, all this is being supported by the steady growth in the coverage of mobile cellular networks.

The International Telecommunication Union estimates that the low and middle-income countries of the world have over 70% of the five billion wireless subscribers overall. The GSM Association confirms that over 85% of the world's population can access commercial wireless signals, a feat even the electrical grid has found difficult to achieve.

Patients in under-served areas of both developing as well as developed countries can overcome human resource shortages in the health sector. They can use the video, imaging, data, text or voice functions of a mobile device to communicate or consult a health professional. This is applicable in other situations also such as for management of chronic diseases of patients unable to leave home.

SOCIAL MEDIA IS BRINGING IN NEW COMMUNICATIONS LANDSCAPES IN HEALTHCARE

In most of the world, people's perception of the healthcare industry is marred with mistrust and doubt. Several factors have led to this chronic viewpoint — lack of transparency, avoidable harm to patients, endless red tape, unnecessary care, widespread inefficiencies, wasteful spending and ceaseless intrusions from drug cartels.

For the first time, this new communication tool is helping patients engage positively and proactively with healthcare organizations. By identifying negativity, social media is helping to address the concerns and complaints, while harvesting positive sentiment.

All over the world, more and more people are increasingly turning to digital tools for maintaining their overall health. According to a recent Pew Research Center study, nearly 33% of American adults turn to the web for figuring out a medical issue, and an overwhelmingly large number of patients prefer digital health communications. However, of all the hospitals in the US, hardly 26% were active on social media.

According to a recent Price Waterhouse Cooper's report, patients are more trustful of social media communications from doctors rather than from drug companies, health insurers or hospitals. That indicates clinicians are still the central reference for patients, while remaining at the focus of communication models. However, considering the number of practicing physicians, very few of them are active on social media. Moreover, providers and physicians prefer to talk more among themselves via social media, rather than directly to the patients.

One of the spectacular ways social media is shaping communications can be seen in the formation of patient groups. Moreover, such patient groups are demanding a more meaningful role and greater transparency in patient/provider relationships. The relationship between providers and patients is also undergoing a sea change with people able to access more information on the web very easily. People are beginning to realize that several providers are inadequately prepared to deal with their request for information due to malpractice claims and HIPAA laws.

HOW ARE HOSPITALS USING DIFFERENT CHANNELS FOR IMPROVING COMMUNICATIONS?

Hospitals are finding that locating clinicians and knowing how and when they can communicate cuts down time loss dramatically. Unified communications with integrated collaboration and information technologies offers a key area for improvement in opportunities. Time-sensitive interactions through better communication technologies can help both the originator and the recipient of the communication.

Although the vast range of communication and information technologies available may contribute to communication complexity, hospitals are finding that they need health system wide technology portfolios while integrating with the improvements in technology.

No magic pill exists for providing a cure for a hospital struggling with communication challenges. However, with the right mix of technologies and changes in process, caregivers can communicate more efficiently and effectively. This will allow them to focus more on providing outstanding patient care.

UNDERSTANDING COMMUNICATION SYSTEMS WITHIN HEALTHCARE

Normally, communication systems within healthcare include people, messages, organizational structures and mediating technologies. Moreover, these systems may use formal or informal structures when supporting communication needs.

To start with, the channel forms the pipe along which messages are exchanged. These channels may be of a wide variety, ranging from the basic face-to-face conversations to telecommunication channels such as telephonic conversations or e-mail exchanges and computational channels such as the medical records. Channels are associated with attributes such as capacity and noise and these determine their suitability for different tasks. In addition, channels can be synchronous or asynchronous.

Telephones are an example of the commonest form of two-way synchronous communication channels – two parties can exchange messages across the channel at the same time. However, synchronous channels can be interruptive, with the interruptions having the capacity of creating a negative impact on individuals with high cognitive loads. For example, a clinician may have forgotten to carry out a clinical task because a telephone call had interrupted him when he was busy.

Individuals separated in time typically use asynchronous channels to communicate. Due to lack of simultaneous communication, they resort to a form of conversation based on a series of message exchanges. Some examples of this type of communications are Post-It notes left on the desk of a colleague and electronic messaging systems. The major advantage of asynchronous communication is that it is inherently non-interruptive, with the busy individual having a choice of ignoring non-urgent communication until a more convenient time.

In healthcare, the sender structures messages with an aim of achieving a specific task while using available resources to suit the needs of the receiver. There can be informal messages with variable structures that use voice and electronic messages, whereas formal or structured communication use formats such as hospital discharge summaries. Some of these messages may also be computer generated and typically following standard formats such as HL7, which is now the international messaging standard followed within healthcare.

Communication within healthcare can also be defined by formal procedures or policies as opposed to being governed by technology. There can be different policies within a hospital to define communication system performance, without being tied to any specific technology. For example, the policy may not allow a general practitioner to access medical records directly from the records department without the permission of the clinician.

Different information transactions may involve agents that build up the communication system. For example, a ward clerk fielding all telephone calls in a busy clinical unit. Here, the hospital's policy has created an organizational structure in the form of the clerk's specific communication role, which allows minimum interruption to the clinical staff. However, agents are required to have attributes such as understanding of language and specific tasks.

In communication systems within a hospital, the same channel can be used to handle different kinds of communication services. For example, the telephone line, although used primarily for voice communication, also serves for fax transmission and reception. Another example is a mobile phone being used for text messaging, image transmission in addition to providing voice-mail.

Hospital staff may use different communication devices to run communication systems. For example, a doctor may need to use a personal digital assistant, a fax machine and a telephone. Mostly, different tasks and situations call for the use of different devices. Sometimes, communication devices are small enough to be worn as personal accessories, such as patients wearing heart rate monitors and blood-pressure monitors.

Interaction mode is an important way in which interactions within a healthcare unit can be designed. For example, some communications may be very urgent and demand immediate attention – through the ringing tone of a mobile phone, while others are designed not to interrupt – a text message. However, the receiver may choose to convert the asynchronous service designed not to interrupt, to an interruptive interaction mode, such as by turning on the notifications on his or her mobile to generate a tone when a text message arrives. Of course, this alters the impact of the service on the message receiver.

In any healthcare unit, patient privacy concerns mandate that security protocols be followed so that unauthorized personnel cannot access clinical records. Communication systems may protect privacy by encoding messages to prevent them from being intercepted and interpreted by unscrupulous individuals. Similarly, medical reports sent over emails may be encrypted, so that only the recipient, who possesses a special key, can open, decode and read them. Usually, the choice of security protocol used depends on the degree of risk attached to unauthorized access of the message content.

CONCLUSION

The communication system used in a healthcare unit is largely dependent on the hospital - whether it is adequately prepared to take on positive and negative patient communication, on social media and on other channels. While larger hospitals can involve staff and resources to monitor and respond to positive and negative comments regularly, smaller healthcare units may not have adequate resources to respond timely. Hospitals with tighter budgets may have to revert to using free tools for monitoring social media to record patient sentiment.

REFERENCES

mHealth New horizons for health through mobile technologies
http://www.who.int/goe/publications/goe_mhealth_web.pdf

Social Media And Healthcare: Navigating The New Communications Landscape
http://binaryfountain.com/social-media-and-healthcare-navigating-the-new-communications-landscape/

Communication Systems in Healthcare
http://www.ncbi.nlm.nih.gov/pmc/articles/PMC1579411/

HEALTH MANAGEMENT INITIATIVES WITH BIG DATA AND ANALYTICS CAPABILITY

Data is growing at an exponential rate. Estimates are that more than 90% of the total information in this world came into existence in only the last two years. The current rate of data creation is about 2.5 quintillion bytes per day Taking into account all the cell phone GPS signals, purchase transaction records, digital pictures and videos, posts to the social media sites, sensor data used to gather climatic and health information to name only a few, all these constitute big data.

This huge quantity of data needs expert management to be handled with order. For example, the Watson Foundations is a platform developed by IBM for handling enterprise class big data and analytics such as those to be found in healthcare. With a modern Information Management architecture, Watson Foundation helps organizations look for fresh insights, operate in real-time and establish trust with patients.

TECHNOLOGIES MAKING UP THE BIG DATA AND ANALYTICS CAPABILITIES

Data Management and Warehousing capabilities allow improved performance when working with multiple workloads that are common in healthcare. This helps to lower costs and deployment times related to storage, administration, development and server deployments. The overall operational speed improves as the capabilities are optimized for analytics workloads.

The Apache Hadoop System offers improved performance and security features, development tools, visualizations, analytics and application accelerators, when handling large amounts of data.

Stream Computing offers real-time and efficient analytic processing when capturing and analyzing data in volumes. Healthcare information is dynamic and requires descriptive and predictive analytics for supporting real-time decisions. With stream computing, analytics happens constantly and instantly, leading to lowered storage capacity requirements. This allows healthcare professionals to analyze more and make better decisions faster.

Content Management is an extremely important tool for healthcare organizations dealing with huge quantities of information. Content management provides a cost-effective control for the comprehensive management of documents and content life cycle. Existing and newer content can be handled with scale, security and stability.

Information Integration and Governance is necessary as healthcare institutes generate a large variety of documents including reports, images, charts and many more. In most cases, several types of documents need to be integrated together for proper understanding, managing and governing healthcare required by patients. Moreover, these documents may have varying life cycles.

HEALTHCARE PAYERS BENEFIT FROM BIG DATA

Business models for healthcare payers such as for insurers and others are undergoing seismic changes. Business models are transitioning to relationships that are more member-centric. New provider models such as the Accountable Care Organizations are being introduced. New acts are being implemented such as the Healthcare Information Exchanges and the Affordable Care Act.

With all these large-scale transformations involving the healthcare business, this industry is facing several challenges as well as opportunities for improving patient outcomes, generating revenue and reducing costs. However, the capability of an organization to take advantage of Information Management regarding big data will define the extent of objectives it can realize from the opportunities presented. By capturing, integrating and integrating large amounts of information sets, healthcare institutions can:

- Improve their clinical outcomes, while ensuring quality and efficiency.

- Analyze patient characteristics vis-a-vis the cost of treatment and outcomes. This will be instrumental in identifying the most effective treatment both clinically as well as from cost considerations.

- Apply advanced analytics to patient profiles such as predictive modeling and segmentation. This will allow identification of patients suitable for and benefiting from preventive care and or lifestyle changes.

- Offer tools and analysis for influencing the behavior of providers.

- Profile diseases on a broader scale for identification and prediction of events to support initiatives for prevention.

- Provide support for participatory healthcare by collecting and publishing data on medical procedures. This will help patients in determining what care regimen or protocol could offer them the best value.

- Support health initiatives to improve outcomes. Payers often offer mobile applications to help patients improve their health by managing their care and by locating providers.

- Collect data from such mobile interactions. Analysis of the collected information can help payers monitor adherence to drug and treatment regimens. They can also detect trends that are leading to the wellness of individuals and the population.

- Identify, predict and minimize fraud by implementing systems for advanced analytics such as techniques for machine learning, for detection of fraud and for checking the consistency and accuracy of claims.

- Authorize nearly real-time claims such as those authorized by credit cards.

- Create new revenue streams from third parties by providing them with aggregated and synthesized clinical records and claims datasets of patients. As an example, payers can license their data to third parties. They in turn can assist pharmaceutical companies in identifying patients for inclusion in clinical trials.

WHAT ARE THE CHALLENGES OF BIG DATA IN HEALTHCARE?

The exponential growth of data is expected to take the currently estimated 50 petabytes of data that healthcare generates today to about 25,000 petabytes by 2020. Although healthcare payers already store and analyze a large part of this data for reviewing and settling claims, they are yet to come up to the level where they can provide analytic insight. For that, payers would need to increase the scope of the information collected.

Payers already collect provider information, the clinical/medical data in the form of electronic health records. They collect this through reciprocal arrangements with HTEs and providers.

Several analysis scenarios would benefit from social data related to patient/member behavior. Consumer information and feeds from various social media sites can indicate important trends and opinions, while acting as potential grounds for testing hypothesis.

A broad base of demographic, epidemiological and medical information can be found in the huge amounts of data related to public and population health published by government sources such as the Center for Medicare and Medicaid Services, health.gov, National Institutes of Health and many others.

Pharmaceutical and medical product manufacturers are publicly releasing increasing amounts of data related to research and development including clinical trials. A growing number of third parties as information aggregators are collecting healthcare related data and synthesizing it for profit.

For stakeholders, the challenge lies in their current inability to analyze these vast amounts of highly complex data cost effectively. There are several reasons for this, such as data coming in from multiple sources and in incompatible formats. Additionally, the analytical tools currently available are not sophisticated or powerful enough for the purpose.

Healthcare IT often faces conflicting priorities such as demonstrating meaningful use, preparing for ICD 10 and establishing health insurance exchanges. Analytics of big data becomes and additional challenge, especially when it is not a mandate or a regulatory requirement.

Understanding of the power of big data and analytics has not yet permeated deep within the healthcare industry. According to the IT survey of the Global Technology and Industry Research Organization, only about 70% of the payers and about 33% of the providers were aware of big data and the way it is defined.

HOW DOES BIG DATA IMPACT PATIENTS IN HEALTHCARE?

Big data is actually creating a win-win situation for both patients and healthcare systems by defining what is right or appropriate for a patient and what is necessary for the healthcare ecosystem. It is driving a holistic, patient-centered framework that is looking at key pathways to value. The concept is that value is derived from the balance of what the patient spends for his healthcare and its outcome on the patient. With big data, the system-wide improvement can be seen in several ways:

Patients are encouraged to make lifestyle choices that help them remain healthy. In turn, patients build value by taking active roles in their own treatment.

Patients are given the timeliest and appropriate treatment available. The right care requires a coordinated approach across providers and settings. All caregivers work with the same information focusing towards the same goal of avoiding suboptimal strategies and duplication of efforts.

Professionals best matched to the task treat patients to achieve the optimum outcomes. This involves not only the physician, the nurse or assistants, but also the specific selection of the provider.

Healthcare stakeholders such as providers and payers continuously strive to enhance healthcare value while preserving or improving its quality. That could include improving the cost-effectiveness of care, tying provider reimbursement to patient outcomes or eliminating abuse, waste or fraud in the system.

Stakeholders strive to identify new therapies and approaches for delivering care. They use big data to find opportunities to improve for example, clinical trials, surgeries involving births and inpatients and protocols for a particular disease.

Senior Leaders Can Initiate Health Management Initiatives with Big Data and Analytics

Guiding principles that are applicable to other industries are equally valid for healthcare. Senior leaders play a big part here for initiating and advancing health management with big data and analytics:

- Prior to pursuing big data, concentrate on improving the core business.

- Make a personal commitment to play and win.
- Pursue transparency efforts and encourage it as a cultural norm.
- Allow business units and functions to operate with a top-down vision and stimulate innovation from bottom-up.
- Focus on setting increasingly complex goals for big data implementation and concentrate on achieving them over different time horizons – short, medium and long-term.
- Establish successful internal and external communication systems to ensure total alignment.
- Define the appropriate talent strategy and the organizational and leadership model.

REFERENCES

IBM big data and information management
http://www-01.ibm.com/software/data/bigdata/

The 'big data' revolution in healthcare
http://www.google.co.in/url?sa=t&rct=j&q=&esrc=s&source=web&cd=4&ved=0CDsQFjAD&url=http%3A%2F%2Fwww.mckinsey.com%2F~%2Fmedia%2Fmckinsey%2Fdotcom%2Fclient_service%2Fhealthcare%2520systems%2520and%2520services%2Fpdfs%2Fthe_big_data_revolution_in_healthcare.ashx&ei=rqfqVNeNI42JuAS9s4LYCQ&usg=AFQjCNFIpUfpqQQcDlpSXHwco5atclHrag&sig2=F42fol3XEsuKVdX2IUpSLg&bvm=bv.86475890,d.c2E

Accountable Care Drives Big Data and Analytics
http://h20195.www2.hp.com/v2/getpdf.aspx/4AA4-3874ENW.pdf?ver=1.0

Big Data and Healthcare Payers

http://knowledgent.com/whitepaper/big-data-and-healthcare-payers/

MULTIPLE SECURITY STRATEGIES THAT SUIT HEALTHCARE OPERATIONS

Healthcare organizations have come a long way. For them, it has been a multi-pronged approach having to adapt to several changes simultaneously. Primarily, they had to adjust to advances in diagnostic and therapeutic procedures, while conforming to administrative change requirements to meet managed care and at the same time, deal with emerging new technologies in information handling.

Although advances in diagnostic and therapeutic procedures are ongoing and healthcare organizations have been adapting to them with the usual efforts, conforming to necessary administrative changes and handling information technologies is currently the new challenge for the healthcare industry.

With consumers increasingly empowered from accessing the capabilities of the Internet, healthcare industry has been forced to undergo profound changes in organizational structures and processes. As information exchange becomes increasingly dynamic, traditional organizational hierarchies break down, resulting in adoption of newer operational strategies. This brings in dramatic changes in mechanisms of management operations, modes of service delivery and ultimately, in the model of the healthcare business itself.

With far-reaching implications, these changes are still evolving. In the near future, Internet applications that are more advanced are expected to appear. Healthcare operations need to prepare now to evaluate the implications and potential of these new Internet technologies, making it easier to adopt them to local conditions and requirements. They should also plan to demonstrate the value of their efforts by minimizing the risks associated when deploying new products and services using suitable multiple security strategies.

TREMENDOUS CHALLENGES FOR HEALTHCARE

Several factors are contributing to the unprecedented data growth. Major among them is Meaningful Use driving healthcare towards a paperless environment. Additionally, newer methods are evolving in the fields of clinical imaging and diagnostic testing. Data explosion is also attributed to implementation of ICD-10 and use of advanced remote monitoring systems, making it a tremendous challenge for healthcare.

Along with the exponential growth in data generation, internal business needs and Federal regulations demand long-term retention. These requirements bring in additional challenges in the form of expenses and creation of storage capacity. With stiff fines being levied by the Department of Health and Human Services for loss of information, the healthcare sector is beset with even more stringent challenges related to data governance and its protection.

For long-term retention of the huge volume of data being generated, healthcare providers need to adopt better strategies for information protection. To remain one step ahead of the regulatory challenges facing proliferation of information, a strong governance framework is necessary. This will help the healthcare sector transform itself from being data silos to deployment of enterprise-wide information management.

The 2014 report of the HIMSS Analytics presented best practices for addressing the growth of healthcare data and its protection in the long run. According to this report, multiple security strategies should be adopted in the areas of data storage, its backup, archiving and disaster recovery for business continuity.

DEFINING SECURE STRATEGIES FOR DATA STORAGE

Proliferation of healthcare applications and the data associated with them are one of the key factors involving exponential growth in information generation. Involving both small and large bed segment hospitals, such applications include operational, administrative, financial and clinical systems.

Health systems have multiple inventories of applications that require reliable estimates for data growth and storage. Apart from the primary applications and data types, healthcare has additional sources generating new data. Prevalent among these are from newer technologies such as proteomics, biometric sensors, digital pathology and genomics. As technology advances, it will continue to impact future data growth.

With increasing growth and compilation of data volume, storage and archival planning assumes greater importance. By thinking long-term, healthcare systems can determine projections for data growth over, say, the next five years. This requires developing an effective strategy for management of information by understanding the evolution of data storage over time along with the associated infrastructure requirement.

A health system generates data in multiple formats with different requirements between applications. Developing an effective strategy for management of data in a hospital involves the IT organization addressing variable storage needs, the need to access, speed of access and cost implications for the growing amounts of data generated.

DEFINING BACKUP STRATEGIES FOR STORED DATA

Developing backup strategies for storing data safely should begin with a preliminary review of the backup processes and policies existing currently. The review should cover all applications and data types to determine what needs to be backed up, the nature of the backup required and the duration of storage.

One of the challenges facing implementers of backup solutions is that healthcare information exists on several endpoints such as desktops, servers, mobile and wearable devices and virtualized machines. Each of these environments requires the use of different backup solutions – increasing the time spent in managing the backup, involves more resources and adds expenses for the business.

General perception towards the backup process also hampers an effective implementation of the backup strategy. Backup is generally perceived as a resource-hungry process making machines run slower. Therefore, to make daily operations more efficient, it is essential to classify data and introduce clarity in terms of storage and access requirements and risk management. Typical classification begins with segmenting stored data into backup and archival types.

Static data that is seldom accessed and updated less frequently is better suited for storage in the archives. On the other hand, data being accessed and updated more frequently is typically dynamic and needs to be kept in backup. Recovery times and recovery point objectives are shorter for backup data. The backup strategy should define when and under what conditions backup information is to be treated as archival data.

DEFINING BACKUP MEDIA AND TECHNOLOGIES FOR STORING DATA

For adequate protection of information from several elements, data protection plans should consider storing multiple copies of data onsite and offsite. Proper protection should include an onsite backup along with the original data and an offsite backup copy.

While the offsite backup offers protection from disasters to the facility caused by floods or fires, the onsite backup offers rapid restoration of data. The backup strategy should also include a process for periodically testing the backup and recovery process and training for the staff on methods of responding to and mitigating disasters.

Currently, two models are popular for storing data for backup and archiving. While a networked cloud provides quicker access with reduced recovery times, it is possible to automate the system of backup on clouds without human intervention. This makes the cloud technology suitable for accessing datasets anytime and from anywhere.

For long-term archival backup, tapes offer good reliability along with a low cost of ownership. Newer tape technology is making them more reliable while increasing their access speeds and capacity in comparison to SATA disk drives. Backup strategies should also include processes for tiring of data and removal of inactive information from the archival streams, thereby allowing healthcare organizations to meet their SLAs.

DEFINING ADMINISTRATIVE SAFEGUARDS

Healthcare facilities are required to have administrative policies and procedures that safeguard and protect the privacy, security and confidentiality of their patients' PHI or data. Both, the HIPAA Security Rule and the HIPAA Privacy Rule advocate this.

For maintaining the security within the system, it is very important to assess the risk of unauthorized disclosure or use of data. It is necessary that healthcare comply with Meaningful Use requirements.

Facilities that store PHI or health IT data and hardware that is used to access them need physical safeguards, because the security of health information can be physically threatened whether it is in paper or electronic formation. Although most safeguards for both are common across different industry sectors, some procedures and policies are unique to healthcare alone.

Access control for healthcare facilities – Limiting physical access to facilities housing the health IT for unauthorized personnel.

Access control for workstation use and security – Specify appropriate use for the workstations while restricting access to workstations that handle PHI.

Control over device and media – Restrict the entry, use and exit of hardware and electronic media containing PHI to and from the facility. Control the accountability and movement of such items within a restricted area, including data backup and storage, disposal and reuse.

DEFINING TECHNICAL SAFEGUARDS

Health IT systems need to protect their patients' PHI by building technical safeguards to limit the access to electronic information. Not only should there be measures to limit physical access, processes and procedures need to be in place to ensure data is encrypted and decrypted. Data is most vulnerable when being transmitted to others. Therefore, unauthorized access to data must be guarded against when it is in transit.

Healthcare systems should have the following elements of technical safeguards in their procedures and policies -

- Access rights to data or PHI – Equip software programs or persons with appropriate access rights such as unique user identification protocols, automatic logoff, emergency access controls and procedures and appropriate encryption and decryption mechanisms.

- Security during transmission – ensure adequate guards are in place to thwart unauthorized access to data being transmitted over any communications network.

- Audit and Integrity control – Protect PHI from improper use, alteration or destruction by recording and examining health IT system activity. Include and implement mechanisms for authenticating PHI.

- Proof of identity – Use mechanisms to verify that an entity or person seeking access to PHI is actually what or who they claim to be.

CONCLUSION

Although setting up and implementing multiple safeguards and security strategies do actually work, it is important that the healthcare sector does not become complacent. Strategies need to be regularly put to test for verifying their efficacy, and if required, adequately updated. Attackers are forever experimenting with newer sophisticated ways of penetrating networks. Even if automated security measures are in place, they will never be foolproof. Security strategies will require constant supervision and evaluation to allow them to continue being effective.

REFERENCES

Security School: Data protection strategies for health care

http://searchhealthit.techtarget.com/feature/Security-School-Data-protection-strategies-for-health-care

Information Protection Framework: Data Security Compliance and Today's Healthcare Industry

http://www.business.att.com/content/whitepaper/seccon_infoproframework.pdf

A Healthier Practice Through Effective Backup

http://www.hitechanswers.net/backup-essential-to-technology-strategy/

Best Practices for Health IT Data Management
http://www.ironmountain.com/Knowledge-Center/Reference-Library/View-by-Document-Type/Best-Practices/H/Health-IT-Data-Management.aspx#sthash.xVKYxoEr.dpuf

Networking Health: Prescriptions for the Internet.
http://www.ncbi.nlm.nih.gov/books/NBK44715/

How Do I Ensure Security in Our System?
http://www.hrsa.gov/healthit/toolbox/HIVAIDSCaretoolbox/SecurityAndPrivacyIssues/howdoiensuresec.html

POST EHR-ERA IN THE HEALTHCARE INDUSTRY

According to the latest report from IDC Health Insight, care delivery is in for big changes in the near future. This includes a reshaped role for Electronic Health Records or EHRs. Hospitals that were sharply focused on complying with meaningful use are now expanding on the use of EHR and related functionality to reach the next step – exploring options of infrastructure and platform to augment practicality.

Hospitals are now aiming to go beyond the basic EHR and their offerings. Their main aim is to meet the needs of their work flow that accountable care has changed. Therefore, by pulling away from a focus centered on EHR applications, the healthcare industry has a broader IT ecosystem in sight. Starting with backup and disaster recovery solutions, hospitals now need to store clinical and imaging data in environments that will organize and centralize the information as well.

THE FATE OF FIRST-GENERATION EHRS

After having implemented the full functionality of an EHR system, most US providers feel their EHR systems suppliers cannot supply the type of tools needed to restore productivity. To them, EHR is becoming more of a simple app, especially when what they actually require is coordinated communication and care. Therefore, in places where providers are working, EHR is unable to provide them functionality.

The above situation is leading to a second-generation of EHRs replacing those of the first-generation. These newer EHRs can work on broader platforms, with more apps and have more capabilities. Additionally, hospitals are also incorporating the newer EHRs into larger IT initiatives. This allows them to use better apps for specific care situations and populations by going beyond the functionality of the EHR. Providers now realize that the EHR is not and cannot be the ultimate for care delivery.

THE ONWARD MARCH OF HEALTHCARE INDUSTRIALIZATION

So far, healthcare has always been a one-off experience with an individual patient. However, that is fast changing with industrialization of healthcare. With newer approaches to care delivery, outcomes are uniform and care is moving towards a set of standardized processes where the interaction with the patient is repeatable.

With industrialization of healthcare, hospitals are able to provide better quality of care and at the same time, ensure improved productivity for providers. Overall, healthcare delivery has now begun to create some value.

RIDING ON THE HEALTHCARE CLOUD

The healthcare industry is creating care communities that have accountable delivery systems and gel very well with cloud services. Although security issues have been hounding cloud services so far, actual practice has proven them largely unfounded. Hospitals have come to realize that clouds can offer them better security than what they themselves could achieve by on-site deployment.

With security in cloud not being a concern any longer, thanks to the HIPAA omnibus rule and the ability of the providers to sign

BAAs, cloud adoption is flourishing. Healthcare industry IT ecosystem is increasingly using virtualization, storage and desktop servers in hospitals even when all their EHR data is stored on-site. These organizations are creating an architecture pathway before they move their new capabilities on to clouds.

ANALYZING THE CRITICALITY OF ANALYTICS

Cost accounting and activity based costing remain the major concerns of almost all hospitals. Currently, these processes are not available widely, resulting in providers being unable to understand their costs. Performance analytics are also not as precise as they should be, and providers are still getting their acts together with financial and clinical analysis.

Hospitals are still in a learning phase - trying to identify and understand the outcomes of high-risk patients. They need specific analytic tool sets to keep track of certain patients so that they can reach out to the population. Such analytic application tools are also necessary for collaborating and communicating. For example, they are needed to share patient documentation across a health system and to aggregate and generate reports for identifying gaps in health care.

REALIZING PERSONALIZED CLINICAL DECISION SUPPORT

In the future, healthcare may involve personalized medicine – care based on genetic data and involving genomics. For the present, however, healthcare is moving clinical decision support away from the rules-based system. Most rules-based clinical decision support systems are generalized and do not reflect the medical history of a specific patient.

Therefore, hospitals are moving towards clinical decision support systems that really check the history of a patient and raise the alarm only when appropriate. This process is expected to become increasingly more customized while reflecting its multi-factorial analysis.

The system will be able to provide recommendations for clinical decision support that are specific, and originate from the clinical data and guidelines of the organization, the medical history of the patient, scientific and medical literature, best practices and guidelines from medical boards and other organizations.

Such detailed, personalized, patient-specific recommendations will make the clinical decision support more useful and providers are more likely to accept them.

MAKING REVENUE CYCLE MANAGEMENT MISSION CRITICAL

Although ICD-10 is causing many changes in healthcare, managing the revenue cycle is going to make it better still. For example, customers do not better their service experience when they receive a bill with a huge amount, a month after their discharge and containing something they are unable to comprehend what they are paying for.

Therefore, hospitals are changing their revenue cycles to let patients know up front what costs are applicable to them. By discussing with patients about the costs, they will understand the different treatment options available along with the financial impact expected. This is expected to be specifically helpful to high-deductible patients and those who will self-pay.

Hospitals are also looking at concurrent coding. They realize that it is really important to get the bills out quicker and to be able to provide estimates before people agree to treatment and care. Along with ICD-10, hospitals are trying for computer assisted coding within the current generation of revenue cycle management systems in addition to clinical documentation improvement programs.

CONTINUING TO DO BUSINESS WITH UNDERINVESTMENT

Providers are at crossroads right now. On one hand, they have invested in EHRs and started to depend on them. On the other, they are still not ready to let go of their on-site storage systems, since they have not yet invested in cloud service infrastructure. This is leading to a situation where the hospital has to stop work when systems break down. Because of staff turnover and organization restructuring, fewer staff in the hospital now know the process as it was done on paper.

This makes it very inconvenient for providers as they have come to depend on EHRs and cannot afford downtimes. The situation also affects patient safety, as going back to the paper processes is not a well-ensured path. Therefore, it is very necessary that providers start investing in tools for data recovery and business continuity - at least, until they are ready to use the cloud services.

Investment in business continuity becomes unavoidable, as providers grow more dependable on EHRs and other clinical applications that require more frequent replication. Providers need to test their systems to make sure they are confident of what to do when things go wrong. They need to ensure continuity of delivery of safe and quality care in spite of network problems.

MOVING TO THE PRIVATE CLOUD

With better support and security from the private cloud services, hospitals are finding they incur more expenses if they set up their own data storage on-site. Apart from the infrastructure and technology setup, they require an expert IT team as well, who must be trained regularly to keep them up to date. This is an area outside the core competence of a healthcare system.

Private cloud, on the other hand, can provide better security, scale of operation and allow the hospital staff to focus on their core competency – that of providing care. Additionally, private cloud, apart from solving the privacy and security issues, reduce the risk for the hospital and all this, at a lower cost than what the hospital could have done on their own.

SELECTING A SUITABLE PRIVATE CLOUD

Private cloud vendors must also take steps to gain the trust of healthcare providers and payers by taking on a greater responsibility for protecting the privacy of patient data. Vendors that need to share healthcare data in environments such as hybrid clouds will do well to re-assess their HIPAA policies and procedures completely and ensure they can meet the newer, more stringent requirements.

Vendors must also conduct independent audits using external consultants. They must ensure they are in compliance by reviewing their policies and procedures regularly. While healthcare organizations must share data among other entities to support their accountable care initiatives or HIE activities, private cloud vendors must provide the ability to share data while keeping PHI private – this is now a business imperative.

CONCLUSION

According to the Covisint study conducted by Porter Research, more than half the leading healthcare executives of the nation placed high importance in cloud-based technologies, even though more than 70% of the industry is still paper-based.

That goes to show that healthcare CIOs are now trusting and embracing the cloud, thereby helping the industry transform the business and deliver accountable care.

REFERENCES

Entering a new era of population health
http://www.healthcareitnews.com/news/entering-new-era-population-health

Population health success depends on good data
http://www.healthcareitnews.com/news/population-health-depends-good-data

New to-do lists loom for 'post-EHR era'

http://www.healthcareitnews.com/news/
new-do-lists-loom-post-ehr-era

Has the cloud found its moment?

http://www.healthcareitnews.com/news/
has-cloud-found-its-moment

KNOWLEDGE AND QUALITY OF HEALTHCARE DATA AND INFORMATION

Facilitating healthcare data transitions from paper to electronic systems depends on how standards, education, research and technologies will capture, use and maintain the information accurately. Transforming healthcare data into meaningful information is a central concern for the healthcare industry including providers, the government and the consumers.

The American Health Information Management Association or AHIMA wants the healthcare industry to -

- Develop and implement standards for collecting, mapping and documenting data
- Support quality information and data by implementing continual quality improvement strategies
- Quantify the impact of data variability and identify solutions through research
- Collect high quality data at the point of care through proper design of application technology that also supports data aggregation, exchange and retrieval
- Ensure healthcare data quality by educating consumers.

WHY IS QUALITY OF HEALTHCARE DATA SO IMPORTANT?

As the US healthcare system transitions from paper to electronic health records, improving the knowledge and quality of data and information in the system is becoming paramount. It is now evident poor data and information has caused several errors and adverse incidents in healthcare. Apart from threatening patient safety, poor quality of data is very often the cause of increases in healthcare costs, while inhibiting exchange of health information, initiatives of performance measurement and research.

It is likely that the quality of data is essential within the individual organization, but that may not be sufficient. The data quality model may work for a healthcare enterprise that integrates multiple systems. However, it may not work when the same data is shared between applications within the organization. This is because such integration requires a meta data approach according to specified enterprise data standards.

Another issue facing the healthcare industry is data interoperability between enterprises. This can only be solved by healthcare enterprises adopting universally accepted data standards. A number of standards development organizations such as ASTM, HL7, etc. are developing such standards.

According to healthcare quality and safety, the right information available at the right time can support management decisions for the health system along with proper patient care. Interconnected healthcare systems of the future will require a consensus on essential data content and standards for documentation. Furthermore, by continuously managing the quality of content and data standards, healthcare enterprises will be able to ensure that their information is usable and actionable.

HOW IS HEALTHCARE DATA, INFORMATION AND KNOWLEDGE MANAGED?

Data is a congregation of symbols representing objects and events along with their properties. When data has been transformed into something useful, it becomes information. Information has answers for questions such as who, what, where, when and how many. Information helps in deciding what to do, but does not provide answers to how to do it. Knowledge provides answers to the 'how' part of the question, because knowledge has the instructions and expertise.

In the healthcare industry, clinicians need to understand and appreciate the differences and the relationships between data, information and knowledge. This is necessary as this understanding contributes to the effective delivery of care, service management and patient safety.

Patients consult with health professionals because they can improve the health of the individual patient. If the right data and information reaches the right people at the right time and in the right form, it makes a difference in informing decisions. However, when such things do not happen, the consequences can be inefficient use of resources leading to suboptimal care and preventable clinical errors. That also puts a limit on the ability of patients when taking responsibility for their own health and care.

ENSURING THE QUALITY OF DATA AND INFORMATION

Quality of data is critically important, as this alone provides the primary underlying support for healthcare, overwhelmingly an information-driven activity. All its supporting processes, including decision-making and planning, need high-quality data suitable for its intended use.

Clinicians need to provide effective and timely treatment for their patients. For this, they rely on the accuracy of the information available. Therefore, healthcare organizations have a responsibility of ensuring that the data and information they create and use is of the top-notch quality and suitable for both local and national purposes.

When information is of high quality, it leads to better patient care and increased patient safety. Therefore, the quality of information is defined by its accuracy, contemporary and synchronous nature and non-ambiguity. For example, it is usual for a patient's record to be held in different places and most likely in different formats. However, fields that refer to the same entity must be maintained synchronously and remain the same at all locations. This helps in building and accessing a knowledge base of health depending on protocols, guidelines, scientific research and so on – commonly known as Evidence-Based Practice.

EVIDENCE-BASED MEDICINE PRACTICE HELPS IN DECISION MAKING

Clinicians practicing evidence-based medicine use current-best evidence judiciously, explicitly and conscientiously in making decisions to provide care and medicines to individual patients. Typically, they integrate the best available external clinical evidence from systematic research with individual clinical expertise during their practice of evidence-based medicine.

This requires a decision-making approach where the clinician consults with the patient to arrive at an option best suited for the patient, using the best information available. However, with increasingly disparate sources of information being available to both patients and clinicians, it often becomes difficult for decision makers, as there is no guarantee that the best available evidence is the basis of the information they have accessed.

Now, NICE or the National Institute of Clinical Evidence offers a service, the NHS Evidence, providing health and social care practitioners with easy access to high quality information. This web-based service allows patients and clinicians find access and use high-quality evidence and best practices of both clinical and non-clinical types. NHS Evidence collates information from different sources into a central portal assisted by a powerful search engine.

However, the existence of such information services should not absolve the clinician from developing individual skills related to critical appraisal. Neither do such services help the clinician in assessing the quality of a specific research or in understanding the methods and results of that research.

Most research is imperfect, restricted by a specified scope. Although not an exact science, critical appraisal of a piece of research can help in deciding whether it is good enough for making a decision. Therefore, clinicians need to know that different sources of information will each have their own values, strengths and weaknesses. Clinicians will need to develop individual skills when supporting the development and evaluation of clinical guidelines and care pathways. Accessing resources such as NHS Local, NHS Evidence, NHS resources such as NHS library services and using tools such as the Map of Medicine, will help clinicians make informed decisions in circumstances involving individual patients.

PATIENT-CENTERED CARE NEEDS ACCURATE INFORMATION

Citizens will soon be able to access online data relating to all types of NHS performance. For example, one can search for the clinical practice with the best diabetes care in their borough. With all data available to the patients, clinicians will need to understand another important factor – data transparency – a vast field, with benefits and risks for both professionals and patients.

Data transparency involves access and sharing patient records and the knowledge how that affects the system and the consultation. It also involves transactional service for patients. For example, booking appointments and requesting repeat prescriptions. In the near future, it might also extend the ability of patients to add to their record.

Other than direct patient care, the Secondary Uses Service or SUS provides a repository for information on NHS activity. SUS is useful for performance monitoring, reconciliation and payments. This is a data warehouse with access control, containing patient confidentiality data protected by a consistent pseudonym. SUS forms the basis of a wide range of healthcare analysis for the government and the NHS.

Organizations and individuals use SUS data for clinical and management purposes that do not directly involve patient care. This includes public health, clinical audit, healthcare planning, commissioning, performance improvement, benchmarking, research and clinical governance.

Clinicians should be aware of the need for information accuracy, especially with reference to the specific aspects of SUS. They must also have a general understanding of its secondary uses, mainly related to clinical data being used to support research, public health and for management of health services.

It is also important for clinicians to remember that patient data covers the entire data captured and not just what is entered into the clinical systems. They need to understand the implications of aggregating data and information in terms of both the benefits as well as the risks.

CONCLUSION

Most healthcare stakeholders such as policy makers, planners, clinicians and others often resign themselves to using suboptimal or inaccurate information for their decision-making. This is primarily due to organizations facing fiscal restraints and other factors. That changes their primary focus to operational information and day-to-day survival in a fiscally challenging environment. However, taking time to focus on strategic issues and developing new knowledge will pay healthcare enterprises significant dividends when identifying new approaches to greater value for money and in avoiding unnecessary costs.

REFERENCES

Embedding Informatics in Clinical Education

http://www.eiceresources.org/data-information-and-knowledge-management

Time for a Paradigm Shift: Managing Smarter by Moving from Data and Information to Knowledge and Wisdom in Healthcare Decision-Making

http://www.longwoods.com/content/21669

Statement on Quality Healthcare Data and Information

http://library.ahima.org/xpedio/groups/public/documents/ahima/bok1_047417.hcsp?dDocName=bok1_047417

ICD -10 AND MEANINGFUL USE OF ELECTRONIC HEALTH RECORDS

Inconsistent quality and rising costs are only a few of the challenges that the US healthcare system faces regularly. Potentially, use of electronic health records will improve the effectiveness and efficiency of healthcare providers. While ARRA or the American Recovery and Reinvestment Act of 2009 prioritized a national, inter-operable health information system, the bipartisan support from US policymakers sped up its adoption.

The latest figures are detailed in the journal Health Affairs, published by the HHS office of the National Coordinator for Health Information Technology. According to this publication, in 2013, almost 78 percent of office-based physicians had adopted the EHR system in some form, while 59 percent of the US hospitals had adopted it.

ARRA includes several measures for modernizing the infrastructure of the nation, one of them being HITECH or the Health Information Technology for Economic and Clinical Health Act. In turn, the HITECH Act supports the concept of electronic health records and their meaningful use, commonly known as EHR-MU. This is an effort led by ONC or Office of the National Coordinator for Health IT and CMS or Centers for Medicare & Medicaid Services.

According to the HITECH Act, the healthcare delivery system throughout the US should make meaningful use of inter-operable electronic health records, treating it as a critical national goal. It defines meaningful use as using certified EHR technology in a meaningful manner ensuring that there is provision for electronic exchange of health information to improve the quality of care and that the provider submits information on quality of care and other measures to the Secretary of Health & Human Services.

To expand on the concept still further, meaningful use has five priorities based on the health outcome policy -

- Improving the efficiency, safety and quality of health care while reducing divergence
- Interesting patients and families in their health and well-being
- Improving public and population health
- Developing care coordination
- Ensuring adequate security and privacy protection for personal health information

ELECTRONIC HEALTH RECORDS AND INTEROPERABILITY

Hospitals generate health information in one or several encounters with the patient in care delivery settings. They maintain this patient information as EHRs or Electronic Health Records. This data includes patient demographics, problems, vital signs, medication, past medical history, immunizations, progress notes, radiology reports and laboratory data. Clinicians use EHRs to automate and streamline their work flow as EHRs can generate a total history of the clinical encounter faced by the patient, while supporting other activities related to care directly or indirectly. Such activities include outcome reporting, quality management and evidence-based decision support.

HITECH stimulus provisions such as ICD-10 stressing on the meaningful use of EHRs are leading many physicians and hospitals towards adopting EHR systems for modernizing their operations. Along with the increase in EHRs, there is also a need for a sufficiently detailed and expandable standard code set to capture the data from current as well as future healthcare accurately. Therefore, ICD-10 cannot be considered a competing initiative, but an enabler to allow the healthcare industry to adopt EHR for building a data infrastructure. The nationwide healthcare system urgently needs this data infrastructure where pharmacies, laboratories, hospitals and clinicians can share PHI or patient health information electronically and securely.

According to CMS, interoperability can only be achieved effectively with standardized data. This will allow sharing information between different EHR and health plan systems. ICD-10 is one of many classification systems and referencing technologies that provide a uniform way of collecting and maintaining patient data.

In this evolving healthcare market, the emerging health economy is shifting from FFS or Fee-for-Service to P4P or Pay-for-Performance and P4V or Pay-for-Value models. Additionally, business systems impacted by this shift need upgrading and adjusting of associated costs so that they comply with multiple federal initiatives. In this context, the eHealth initiatives put forward by CMS are helping to meet the Triple AIM goals of improvement – leading to an increase in the efficiency of health delivery in the US.

CMS eHealth initiatives aim at improving healthcare delivery using simplified, standardized electronic information and technology. Along with other initiatives for simplification of administration, ICD-10 will improve the quality and efficiency of electronic information exchanged between providers, Medicare and other players.

ICD-10 is instrumental in accelerating research, health status monitoring and in streamlining quality and interoperability. This in turn helps in unifying architectures for public health surveillance leading to an improvement in population health. Interoperability and effective sharing of clinical data requires a common medical language and this is provided by the amalgamation of terminologies and classification systems. Improved patient care coordination across the nation requires secure exchange of information between patients and providers. Initiatives such as eHealth will help advance such requirements.

EHRS, ICD-10 AND MANAGEMENT OF REVENUE CYCLE RISK

Following the newest ICD-10 release announcement, CMS has published ICD-10 testing opportunities for providers still operating with FFS. This is a comprehensive four-pronged approach that tests the Medicare FFS provider for ICD-10 and its preparedness. In this approach, the tests include -

- CMS Internal testing of the provider's claims processing systems
- Downloading CMS Beta testing tools
- Testing the provider's acknowledgements
- Testing the provider end-to-end

Before participating in CMS testing, organizations must first complete their internal testing to ensure that their own systems are operating correctly. This should include Revenue Cycle User Acceptance Testing, as this increases the likelihood of a successful test with CMS. Some lessons learnt from hospitals and health centers across the country employing a variety of strategies to protect revenues during transition to ICS-10 are as follows -

- Ensure representation of all key areas during the planning phase – include payers, charging, billing, IT and coding
- Ensure confirmation of payer requirements before test files are built

- Ensure available resources and time requirements are identified

- Ensure evaluation of test environments to make them available when scheduled for remediation

- Ensure evaluation of a test file for use with different payers

- Ensure validation of a test procedure by starting with a small test file

- Consider if test files will be copied from live billing systems or built manually – reporting trends may be tracked

- Evaluate 835s received from payers for monitoring testing results.

Healthcare organizations striving to manage the impact on resources must include in their initial tests only a limited number of claims with payers as test transactions. This will allow for a shorter learning cycle. For additional testing, it is necessary to include a good cross-section of everyday business as well as coding scenarios related to specialties with expanded code sets. It would be prudent to set the testing team's goal to complete end-to-end testing with all major payers.

Results from the end-to-end testing of the revenue cycle with all major payers, including stakeholders, will be one set of predictors for measuring the impact on KPIs established by the risk management team. By continually monitoring their KPIs, organizations can focus on any delays or interruption of cash flow in accounts receivable to contain or avoid them.

THE ROLE OF LCDS IN PREPARING FOR ICD-10

While preparing for ICD-10 transition, healthcare organizations must not overlook the review of LCDs or Local Coverage Determinations. This allows identification of potential areas of concern that may impact the organization. Regional MACs or Medicare

Administrative Contractors publish LCDs, outlining the coverage and documentation requirements for specific topics. Such documents enumerate where medical necessity may create potential concerns and how the MAC will approach ICD-10 from a coding perspective.

In general, reimbursement is applicable for claim forms that have a diagnosis code listed as supporting medical necessity. By following coding guidelines, the organization presenting the claim form is accurately representing the medical condition of the patient as documented in their records for the service they are reporting.

However, LCDs provide more information, valuable to both the coding and billing staff and the providers, rather than simply a list of diagnosis codes. Each LCD also provides information on the documentation requirements as well as the source documents used for the guidelines. This allows providers to know exactly what is to be documented to demonstrate medical necessity for a specific study or procedure.

Moreover, LCDs allow providers to evaluate the timeliness of the standards of practice they are using to determine the guidelines. For example, a provider may strongly disagree with an LCD, thereby taking up the first steps towards revision of an outdated LCD. If a MAC decides they will revise something more than only the ICD-10 codes, they will be following the normal processes for LCD development as outlined in the Medicare Program Integrity Manual.

CMS does not expect all contractors will follow a specific process when finalizing revised or new LCDs. As part of the finalization process, contractors are required to post responses to comments received along with a summary of the comments.

CONCLUSION

Healthcare organizations will require undergoing several changes when implementing ICD-10 for meaningful use of Electronic

Health Records. Among them, revision of LCDs will definitely be a game-changer and it will impact several organizations. Timely identification of areas of concern and attending to them proactively can potentially avoid extra work, denials and loss of revenue after the implementation date of ICD-10.

REFERENCES

Electronic Health Records
http://www.himss.org/library/ehr/

The "Meaningful Use" Regulation for Electronic Health Records
http://www.nejm.org/doi/full/10.1056/nejmp1006114

Use of Electronic Health Records in U.S. Hospitals
http://www.nejm.org/doi/full/10.1056/nejmsa0900592

More physicians and hospitals are using EHRs than before
http://www.hhs.gov/news/press/2014pres/08/20140807a.html

TOOLS AND STRATEGIES FOR QUALITY IMPROVEMENT IN HEALTHCARE

Transforming hospitals and care homes to PCMH or Patient-Centered Medical Homes involves several changes. These include modifications to the care team structure, scheduling systems, work flow and processes among others. By adopting stable QIs or Quality Improvement strategies, staff will gain a specific approach to use along with the necessary confidence and skills in making these changes.

One of the essential parts of QI is measurement – the staff gets a feedback from measurements. All stakeholders such as patients, board members, leaders and providers, including staff, obtain feedback from measurements about the outcomes of the care they provide or receive along with information about how the organization is progressing towards the transformation.

QISCC or Quality Improvement Strategy Change Concept is partly dependent on HIT or Health Information Technology, because information provides the basis of any improvement in quality. With HIT, practices can collect, manage and report data efficiently and accurately. This provides care teams with the information they need for improving outcomes and processes.

WHAT ARE QUALITY IMPROVEMENT STRATEGIES?

A QI strategy undertaken by a PCMH is an approach to change their way of working. The QI strategy provides necessary tools and a framework so that the PCMH can plan, organize and then monitor, sustain and spread the changes. Data collected provides evidence of the improvements made. PCMH can use HIT as a set of sophisticated tools that supports the information needs of the medical home.

BUILDING A QUALITY IMPROVEMENT INFRASTRUCTURE

Building any quality improvement infrastructure begins with establishing a QI policy, outlining the quality goals of the organization and the processes necessary for identifying strategic QI priorities. A successful QI policy will provide a road map for methods the organization will follow to proceed with the QI efforts.

The second step involves defining the roles and responsibilities within the organization. Spell out the names of persons on the QI committee or team. Name those who are responsible for metrics.

In the third step, outline a process for organizing, monitoring and concluding improvement projects.

The next step involves establishing opportunities for all staff to participate in practice-wide QI work. This involves designating time to review and manage QI tools they will use for improvement. The key to establishing a culture of QI within an organization is reviewing and discussing collected data and information.

USING PROVEN QI TOOLS AND STRATEGIES

Once the medical home or practice has installed a QI team in place and has identified the strategic priorities of QI, they can adopt a formal model for QI that includes a measurement strategy.

The Model for Improvement is the most straightforward and prevalent approach. This includes development of a strategy with aims, measures and ideas, and the use of the PDSA or Plan-Do-Study-Act cycle to test and implement changes rapidly. PCMH can use this as a stand-alone approach, or as a companion approach to Lean Methodology and or others.

The first component of the Model for Improvement is establishing Aims, Measurements and Ideas. Aims define what the practice is trying to accomplish. With Measurements, the practice comes to know whether the change has resulted in tangible improvements. Ideas provide new inputs to define changes that could result in improvements.

The second component of the Model of Improvement is the PDSA cycle or Plan-Do-Study-Act cycle that provides the improvement engine or the thought process that the practice can apply for reaching desired improvement levels. The PDSA cycle involves sequential steps such as –

1. Plan – for planning an intervention;
2. Do – for implementing the change on a small scale to test it;
3. Study – for observing, measuring and analyzing the test change;
4. Act – for using the knowledge gained to plan the next step.

Along with the Model for Improvement, the medical home may also implement Lean Methodology as a strategy for quality improvement. Using Lean means being customer-focused and aiming to improve processes by driving out waste activities that do not add value.

Practices successfully use Lean to manage work flow and engage employees, thereby improving processes, clinical quality and reliability. Among key Lean concepts and methods are analyzing value streams and waste reduction, creating visual displays for information and data boards and rapid process improvement workshops.

PCMH TRANSFORMATION AND QUALITY IMPROVEMENT STRATEGY

Regardless of the QI strategy that a practice adopts, using measurement and data for guiding and driving Improvement measures should form an essential part of any PCMH transformation. The practice must select these measures strategically – preferably, clear data definitions that are nationally endorsed and standardized. The measure set chosen should truly reflect the work of transformation to the PCMH.

The practice should balance its resources required for mapping and reporting the measures against the value that the results bring. The data collected should come from a variety of sources. This is easily done if data is collected concurrently, as work progresses. Practices can facilitate this by designing data collection into work flows within their EHRs.

Display collected data as graphic displays – these convey a lot of meaning and most people can easily understand them. Graphically display the data foster engagement of families, patients, staff, providers and senior leaders. Run charts or Line graphs are the most popular type of QI tool for displaying improvement data, as these can tell in an instant if improvements are indeed occurring. Posting displays in high-traffic areas such as patient waiting rooms, staff lounges and on the rear side of bathroom stall doors is one of the ways of making data visible throughout the practice.

Once multiple changes have been tested using the rapid PDSA cycles from the Model for Improvement, those resulting in positive improvements may be implemented in a successful new process or way of working. The next step involves effectively sustaining the new way of carrying out the work.

After ensuring the change is ready for implementation, time must be allowed for experimentation, as this sorts out the teething problems of the new process and builds support among the practice teams. That helps them to experience and understand how the new method is superior. Once established, communicate the benefits of the improved process.

Allow staff involved in the work to identify the essential features of the innovation. Make sure the new method of working is done consistently as part of new standard work – design standardized work processes that will make the new way of doing things unavoidable. That involves including detailed, documented visual systems where staff develop, agree and follow a defined standardized process.

Demonstrating success with data helps in spreading the change throughout the practice, to other parts of the organization or even to other organizations. This requires having champions who tested the changes initially, and who are prepared to help with the spreading by communicating, influencing and training others.

It is also essential to gain the interest and support of key leaders. This requires a plan and resources that can train staff in carrying out the new process. Prepare for sharing and explaining data while simultaneously addressing resistance.

Health Information Technology and Quality Improvement

HIT or Health Information Technology forms the set of advanced tools that reinforce the information needs of work flows within PCMHs. How healthcare teams interact with their patients characterizes a PCMH rather than the technology it uses. However, modern healthcare depends on the availability and accessibility of information that loses value quickly if it cannot be found, is poorly configured or is incorrect.

Supporting the information infrastructure of a PCMH requires complex technical requirements. For reducing waste and improving patient experiences and outcomes, the work flow needs optimization. At the same time, the information flow must also be optimized so that data, on which clinical decisions are based, is available readily, is current and accurate. When deploying HIT and aligning it with overall PCMH transformation, the practices can optimize technology to support the work flows of the PCMH in the best possible way.

HIT forms a part of Quality Improvement Strategy Change Concept because improvement of quality depends on information. The adoption of HIT has increased dramatically in recent years because of federal incentives for the use of EHRs or Electronic Health Records and their meaningful use. Experience suggests that through optimization of HIT, quality and patient safety can be improved, but there is still no evidence to back it up. However, unless practices have plans to take advantage of the power of HIT for improving the efficiency and quality of their operations, they risk being distracted by the complexity of technology and the amount of information it encompasses.

CONCLUSION

By deploying HIT and aligning it with the change concepts of PCMH, practices can optimize their EHRs for supporting PCMH work flows. PCMH functioning depends on eight core processes that HIT supports. If practices optimize these across the organization, they can improve quality and manage cost. This also requires standardization to assure that the goal of each core process is aligned with the strategic goal of the organization. The PCMH will function as intended provided the work flows and HIT functionality of each core process is carefully integrated.

The eight core processes of the PCMH are:

1. Appointment scheduling and care access monitoring;

2. Understanding and defining the patient population of each provider along with the key sub-population;

3. Tracking and defining the care of individual population

and sub-population including abnormal imaging or lab results and referrals;

4. Providing educational material specific to patients;

5. Providing care reminders for individuals;

6. Providing AVS or after-visit-summaries and key information after every visit;

7. Generating action reports for guiding the care management activity of the team and outcomes reports for monitoring population outcomes and the processes of care;

8. Optimizing communications between care teams and patients with technology such as using a patient portal in the EHR.

REFERENCES

Chapter 44 Tools and Strategies for Quality Improvement and Patient Safety

http://www.ncbi.nlm.nih.gov/books/NBK2682/

Quality Improvement (QI) and the Importance of QI

http://www.hrsa.gov/quality/toolbox/methodology/qualityimprovement/

Quality Improvement Strategy

http://www.safetynetmedicalhome.org/change-concepts/quality-improvement-strategy

CLINICAL PRACTICE GUIDELINES FOR EVIDENCE BASED MEDICINE

In recent years, health care is witnessing an increasing emphasis on evidence, based on the dramatic increase in the volume of scientific information. Each year, several thousands of RCTs or randomized, controlled reviews summarize evidence from multiple studies in general medical journals and specialty journals increasingly conduct meta-analysis that quantitatively pool data.

EBM or evidence-based medicine directly links policy decisions and clinical practice to supporting evidence. Public policy and practice guidelines are increasingly focusing attention on EBM. Evidence-based practice guidelines control clinical trials, systematic reviews and pronouncements that guide medicolegal judgments, government decisions about healthcare financing and insurer's decision.

Two factors are responsible for this increased attention to data in health policy settings and clinical practice. First, health care costs have spiraled, pressurizing governments and private health plans to review the appropriateness and effectiveness of utilization of health services. Second, documented evidence has demonstrated substantial variations in the rate with which treatments and procedures are offered to patients with similar clinical profiles but who are separated geographically. This suggests services are under- or over-utilized.

In a large proportion of cases, essential services that patients need to receive are not being provided. Conversely, ineffective services are performed with regularity. Sometimes, services are misapplied to the wrong population or are incorrectly delivered. This is borne out by more than 100,000 deaths every year in the US from frank medical errors.

WHAT IS NEW ABOUT EVIDENCE BASED MEDICINE?

From the times of Ancient Greece and other venerable medical practitioners all over the world, physicians have tried to keep abreast of the latest evidence by engaging in scientific studies. That means medicine has always been evidence-based. The difference between the traditional application of evidence in medicine and EBM is that in EBM, policy links explicitly to supporting data. EBM emphasizes the examination of comprehensive, critical and explicit evidence.

Comprehensiveness is necessary for ensuring that all evidence is considered rather than just those that reflect a selection bias or support a specific viewpoint. Critical appraisal is important for examining the strengths and weaknesses of the study design so that judgments about the evidence can be linked to quality. Explicitness makes the evaluation transparent and allows readers to understand the analysis methods used, the strengths of the evidence, the existing gaps and the rationale for policies or practice recommendations, whether opinion- or evidence-based.

MISCONCEPTIONS ABOUT EBM

Many people believe that EBM resists medical practices that are not proven in an RCT or other study. Others assume that EBM converts clinical practice into cookbook medicine, resisting efforts of clinicians to assert clinical judgment and individualize care.

Although this happens sometimes, EBM does not advocate it and does not defend it either. Many activities followed in clinical practice remains untested under controlled studies. However, one cannot withhold services based on this criterion, as that would be unrealistic and invalid. RCTs are often difficult to design and fund. Moreover, they rely on the outcome measures that very often do not capture the range of benefits and harms associates with interventions.

Most often, available evidence is of poor quality. It may not pass internal validity or external validity. That means the evidence collected may not reflect the extent of the internal clinical settings of the study, or the findings cannot be extrapolated to other patient populations, settings or providers. For a given patient, the best evidence can at best predict only average outcomes. When looking at the bell curve surrounding the mean, where an individual patient will be located on the curve depends on specific variables such as community resources, provider skills, personal circumstances, past medical history, and risk factors.

EBM insists on making these considerations explicit. While not insisting on evidence from RCTs, it does require that the quality and grade of the evidence be stated clearly and evaluated carefully. EBM allows the use of expert judgment and opinions while setting practice policies and it insists on acknowledgments while doing it. EBM supports the disclosure of gaps in the evidence so that research agendas are understood clearly. At the same time, it also calls for attention to design features that should be incorporated in future studies so that deficiencies in current data are addressed. While not underestimating the importance of individualized care, EBM encourages evidence-based determinant factors in practice and policy decisions to maximize effectiveness and equity for all patients.

WHAT ARE EVIDENCE-BASED CLINICAL PRACTICE GUIDELINES?

The Institute of Medicine explains a CPG or clinical practice guideline as a systematically developed statement that assists the patient and the practitioner make decisions appropriate for health care under specific clinical circumstances.

Evidence-based is implied when a document or recommendation is created using the best clinical research findings of the highest value and a transparent and unbiased process of systematic reviews and appraisals. This aids in the delivery of optimum clinical care to patients.

Therefore, evidence-based clinical practice guidelines can be meaningfully explained as a series of recommendations on clinical care, supported by the best available evidence in clinical literature.

ARE EVIDENCE-BASED CPGS SUPERIOR?

From long, there have been uses and abuses of CPGs. Earlier, AAOS developed consensus-driven CPGs to support high-quality care. The consensus-driven process had a panel of thought-leaders on a specific topic, which after a literature review would produce a document or recommendations based on the consensus of the review panel.

Although these position statements on best care were meant to be unbiased, the documents faced opposition. The development process lacked transparency, and the group of experts were biased towards their own methods of treatment. The same literature review derived very different conclusions when taken up by a different group, more consistent with their goals. This was evidence that the approach had a bias and was untenable. Moreover, in many cases, care decisions were based on guidelines that were more oriented towards economic and not quality goals.

Applying techniques of EBM in developing guidelines reduces the role of opinion and bias significantly, thereby raising its value. Therefore, evidence-based CPGs lead to rich scientific literature of clinical medicine that is elevated and evaluated systematically to provide transparency and minimum bias. That makes evidence-based CPGs true instruments of better patient care and superior to CPGs that are not based on evidence.

HOW USEFUL ARE EVIDENCE-BASED CPGS?

Evidence-based CPGs are developed using a transparent and structured process. That makes them easy to use and difficult to abuse. They are helpful in developing quality measures and in supporting referrals when insurance companies question these. Evidence-based CPGs are also useful as education tools for patients. Evidence-based CPGs play an essential role in developing performance measures for pay-for-performance reimbursement programs.

On the national level, evidence-based CPGs are a direct means of quality improvement. On a local level, these society-based authoritative CPGs, when constructed in the manner described above, are useful for informing and influencing hospital guidelines in promoting best practices. Since they minimize the use of opinion-based guidelines, they can be used to challenge payers' decisions that are not based on high-quality evidence.

Evidence-based CPGs also help to relieve the practicing physician of the burden of attempting to read and assess all the information being published in a certain area of practice. Evidence-based CPGs serve to improve patient outcomes, physician performance and promote good clinical practice by reviewing, rating and synthesizing huge amounts of literature and finally, making an unbiased, evidence-based series of recommendations on clinical problems.

PURPOSE OF CPGS FOR EVIDENCE-BASED MEDICINE

CPGs support the decision-making processes in patient care. Over the past few years, there has been a positive movement towards evidence-based healthcare supported by clinicians, politicians and management, all concerned about quality, consistency and costs. Based on standardized best practices, evidence-based CPGs are capable of supporting advancements in quality and consistency in healthcare. In general, the purpose of CPGs can be listed as –

- To set forth suitable care based on the best available scientific evidence and broad consensus;
- To reduce unsuitable variations in practice;
- To provide a more reasonable basis for referral;
- To promote efficient and effective use of resources;
- To promote a stronger focus for continuing education;
- To promote a focus on quality control and audit;
- To highlight deficiencies of existing literature and advise suitable future research.

COMPUTERIZED GUIDELINES

Evidence-based recommendations can be encoded into computerized guidelines that can automatically generate recommendations about medical procedures to be performed – tailored for an individual patient. There are several advantages of computerized guidelines when compared to those offered by paper-based guidelines.

Chief among these is the availability of a readily accessible reference that provides selective access to guideline knowledge. Computerized guidelines help to improve clarity in decision-making criteria and clinical recommendations, while revealing errors in the content. While offering better descriptions of patient states, computerized guidelines also help to propose timely reminders and patient-specific decision support.

CONCLUSION

The future of EBM lies in developing effective plans for transforming evidence into practice. A promising approach is to modify the implementation strategies to match the type of barriers involved. For example, detailing by local opinion leaders and academics when attitudes are the obstacle, modifying office operations, redesigning order forms, skill building, using computerized reminder systems and other prompts to provide reinforcement and decision support tools to enhance implementation. These measures can be used to apply the thriving abundance of data from clinical research to accomplish the promise of EBM for improving the efficacy and equity of health care.

REFERENCES

Defining evidence-based clinical practice guidelines

http://www.aaos.org/news/aaosnow/jul08/research2.asp

Evidence-Based Medicine and Practice Guidelines - An Overview

http://www.medscape.com/viewarticle/409000_7

Evidence-Based Medicine: Do Clinical Practice Guidelines Contribute to Better Patient Care? -- An Expert Interview With Drs. Joseph O. Jacobson and Antonio C. Wolff

http://www.medscape.org/viewarticle/589088

Clinical practice guidelines

http://www.openclinical.org/guidelines.html

CHALLENGES IN MOBILE HEALTH

Advances in mobile health can be estimated from the $750+ million invested in venture capital in companies. Several corporate giants such as Microsoft, Qualcomm, Apple and Samsung are turning out smartphones capable of capturing medical-quality images of the inner ear or measuring blood pressure, creating mobile health products and investing in startups.

The basic idea is to capture all kinds of data for improving health care. The increasing number of smartphones and associated small, inexpensive sensors along with low-energy Bluetooth and analytical software enable patients to play a more active role in their own health. Simultaneously, nurses and doctors can make house calls without leaving their offices.

However, mobile health technology can be tricky to implement. Wristbands for activity tracking, made by one of the most well known firms, had to be recalled after users complained of skin irritation from wearing it. Measuring blood glucose levels without drawing blood, is still not available because of technological difficulties, although this is a desirable feature for people with diabetes.

On the other hand, there have been technological achievements as well. Mobile phones have helped increase activity among patients with diabetes. Activity monitors provided feedback that combined with existing records of patients, while an algorithm determined the text message to be sent to the patients. Those falling behind in achieving their goals received messages of encouragement. Based on location data from the mobile device some patients received information about nearby aerobics classes or about different ways to exercise indoors. After six months, not only was the average patient walking about a mile farther each day, their blood sugar control had improved significantly.

The success of the above program has two sides. Patients are healthier, translating into a lower cost of caring for them for partners. Usually, payoffs for better managing diabetes, a chronic disease, comes over many years. However, in this case, many patients were able to drop their blood sugar and that equates to savings of $1000 to $1200 in doctor visits and other treatments. Since the program costs $300 per patient to run, the return on the program is substantial.

Based on such results, enthusiasts are convinced that mobile technology can successfully overhaul the delivery of health care. They also estimate that mobile technology will offer sufficient financial benefits so that patients and insurers will be convinced to pay for it.

However, patients are not so easily convinced. Although 10 percent of Americans own a type of tracking device to measure the quality of their sleep, calorie intake or monitor the steps they take, more than half of them no longer use devices. Even when there are more than 100,000 mobile health applications available for smartphones, only a few have been downloaded more than 500 times. Additionally, of those who have downloaded such an application, more than two-thirds have stopped using it.

One reason for the slow enthusiasm has been unrealistic expectation from current imperfect technology. For example, simple functions such as step counting lack precision. Another reason is many people lacked motivation and simply did not take to using these devices and applications. Evidently, a well-designed mobile health system does help provided patients use it.

THE MHEALTH MARKETPLACE AND SMARTPHONES

As of 2014, there were upwards of 140 million smartphones in the US and this number is expected to cross the 200 million mark in the next five years. Thousands of applications are fueling this growth, empowering users in their daily lives. Now consumers can conveniently deposit checks, avoid traffic snarls, play games and stay in touch with their friends, all from their handheld convenience.

However, the US healthcare infrastructure has been rather slow in embracing the non-traditional physician-patient encounter. Very few among the US population have ever used telemedicine, one of mHealth technologies. Although solutions are prevalent in other service-based industries such as travel, insurance and banking, the healthcare industry faces several hurdles when implementing mHealth. For example, extremely few numbers of smartphone users have ever received an email or alert directly related to their health.

An insight into the state of mHealth can be gained from existing mHealth apps. These can be divided into three types of encounters:

- The patient initiates and concludes the encounter
- The healthcare provider initiates and concludes the encounters
- Either initiates the encounter, but the other concludes it.

In the first two encounters, either the patient or the physician can utilize technology personally to meet their medical needs. For example, a physician may look up the dose for a medication or the patient may track his or her blood pressure. In both examples, the physician and the patient are not dependent upon each other.

The third encounter is a much tougher model, as some pre-coordination must exist before action can be taken on data being collected. Here, the patient or physician initiates the app use and the other concludes the interaction.

Given the enormous number of medical apps and mobile platforms prevailing, it is hardly surprising that there exists a lack of standardization. For example, a patient may opt to use a diabetes app without consulting or coordinating with their physician. In the next in-person visit, the physician may only be able to adjust the diabetes regimen by reviewing the paper printout that the patient brought. That marginalizes the value of collecting that data in real time. Had the patient and the physician been able to share data in real time, review it and act on it, complications could be prevented before they had time to arise.

The process of adopting mHealth can also run into logistical hurdles with financial ramifications. For example, a primary care professional managing a population of 2,000 patients may not have adequate resources to integrate and act upon daily notifications that could easily run into hundreds. Modern utility grids are designed to adjust their workflow by foreseeing and managing the peaks and troughs of power consumption. However, healthcare practices, especially the brick-and-mortar type, are fragmented and were not initially designed to work in that manner. Moreover, a utility company has financial incentives for delivering energy efficiently – they save money and improve their margins. For healthcare, unfortunately, there are no financial incentives for either the patient or the physician who want to invest their resources into several discrete mHealth solutions.

Most independent physician practices are unable to invest in new infrastructure because they lack resources. A local barbershop would consider it worthless to invest in a special app that costs thousands of dollars only for allowing customers to book online appointments and get reminders when it is already running to maximum capacity. In healthcare also, a family physician practice operating at capacity, will be reluctant to welcome additional patients and risk decreasing its already wafer-thin margins by investing in new services.

PUBLIC HEALTH, LARGE SCALE HEALTH CARE AND MHEALTH

The level of computing capacity available in even basic cell phones and their high penetration makes this a potential technology for creating significant differences to public health and health care delivery. Researchers can use the mHealth technologies to capture multiple sources of health data. This could include, for example, in-depth information about the environment for GWAS or genome-wide association studies; location and travel areas; detailed information about the physical activities of subjects; physiological responses through sensors attached to the body; and activities through text messaging surveys over extended periods of time.

Further, mHealth methodologies with highly accessible data availability can be utilized to alter public health and health care on a large scale. For example, remote areas without easy physical access routes for physicians can be monitored and health care dispensed with through mHealth technologies. Employing mobile tools can decrease the number of people who develop diabetes through ignorance, prevent accidents at home and help remind people to take their medication as scheduled.

More consumers are now aware of and demand health apps and sensors. However, consumers are still in the process of coming to terns regarding the benefits, risks and impact of these apps and sensors on health outcomes – positive, neutral or negative. The main issues hampering the efforts are privacy, confidentiality, regulatory control, protection to the human subject, logistics and interoperability among carriers. For creating safe, scalable and effective health programs, researchers will need to develop and assess the entire spectrum of mHealth technologies.

CONCLUSION

Mobile healthcare offers an important extension to electronic health care. With mHealth, caregivers are able to gain uninterrupted access to the clinical data of their patients and the latest in medical knowledge. Concurrently, patients with chronic conditions can remain under constant observation without leaving their homes. Full-scale implementation of mHealth involves solving critical challenges such as developing better display technologies, establishing interoperability among electronic health records and security controls for mobile devices. It also requires developing smart algorithms for detecting clinically significant events and subsequently informing caregivers.

Mobile health is opening up new opportunities for personalized healthcare and joint decision-making with physician-patient relationships. However, several new challenges are also coming up – ensuring confidentiality of patient data, empowering patients with medical knowledge in everyday language and most importantly, mindset adjustment of both patients and caregivers.

REFERENCES

mHealth - Mobile Health Technologies

http://obssr.od.nih.gov/scientific_areas/methodology/mhealth/

Mobile Technology and Health Care, From NIH Director Dr. Francis S. Collins

http://www.nlm.nih.gov/medlineplus/magazine/issues/winter11/articles/winter11pg2-3.html

Why Mobile Health Technologies Haven't Taken Off (Yet)

http://www.forbes.com/sites/robertszczerba/2014/07/16/why-mobile-health-technologies-havent-taken-off-yet/

Mobile Health's Growing Pains

http://www.technologyreview.com/news/529031/mobile-healths-growing-pains/

PROTECTING AGAINST ANTHEM-LIKE ATTACKS

According to reports, the financial consequence of Anthem's massive data breach is expected to extend beyond the $100-million mark. The American International Group, which leads the cyber insurance policy of the second largest US Health insurance provider, covers losses only up to $100 million. With Anthem catering to more than 80 million customers, staff and investors, this amount may not be enough to contact, reassure and notify them.

WHAT WAS THE ANTHEM BREACH ABOUT?

In a security breach assisted with a stolen password, hackers were able to penetrate Anthem's database and steal upwards of 80 million records. The database held personal information related to employees of Anthem apart from those of their former and current clients.

The President and CEO of Anthem, Joseph Swedish, confirmed that among the stolen data were the names of clients, their dates of birth, physical and email addresses, Social Security numbers and medical Ids. However, investigations have failed to find evidence suggesting the stealth of medical data such as test results and or financial information.

Although Anthem confirmed the data breach around January 29, 2015, they issued the first public warnings on February 4. According to the health insurer, the data breach had started as early as December 10 and the intrusions continued up to January 27, when Anthem first detected suspicious database queries. Investigations later found that the company's automated defenses had already blocked some of these unauthorized data queries from as early as December 10.

In the meantime, Mandiant, a cyberforensic team, is working with Anthem to piece together and analyze the nature of the security failure, while the company is under investigation by the FBI. The Attorney General and the state insurance commissioners have also launched their own investigations into the cyber-attack. In addition, a US Senate committee is looking into how prepared the US healthcare industry is for mitigating such and similar cyber-attacks and threats.

Apart from the loss of data, Anthem will most likely be exhausting its cyber insurance policy because it needs to notify affected customers and that is going to be expensive. Sources from The Insurance Insider confirm that AIG, Lexington, Safehold and Zurich among others, are the authors of Anthem's cyber insurance policy. With Anthem planning to notify every individual affected by the breach, people with questions and queries can contact Anthem on special hotlines.

Along with Anthem, the authors of their cyber insurance policy are also a worried lot, as they could as well be exposed to losses resulting from the breach. One consolation is that so far, there is no clear precedent for such claims.

The near-term implications for Anthem because of this incident will be related to the likely expenses for providing their members with identity protection support. The public will suffer the effects of this breach for a long time, as the attackers will abide their time when abusing certain pieces of the stolen data – the nature of that abuse is unfathomable just yet.

WHY WAS ANTHEM VULNERABLE?

The healthcare sector has increasingly been the target of attackers and hackers. Along with multiple flash alerts being issued by the FBI, there has been a substantial increase in spear-phishing type of attacks on the healthcare industry. Advanced persistent threat attackers often use this type of tactics to steal intellectual property from healthcare firms and medical device manufacturers.

According to investigators, attackers penetrated Anthem's database using a stolen password. Hackers capture such personal information typically via frauds known as phishing. Post the hack, Anthem has been sending out advices and recommendations to its employees. The nature of these security advices is a pointer to what went wrong in the first place.

The health insurance provider recommends its members and employees to not respond to emails that are purportedly coming from Anthem and include "click here" links for monitoring credits. The purpose of these links is to redirect the user to a website controlled by the attacker, where a malicious script takes over. The recommendation is that users should preferably type the address of the website they would like to visit in the browser directly, rather than clicking on the given link.

Anthem has also warned members to beware of responding to callers asking for information about their credit cards, social security numbers or for discussing about the breach – something that the health insurer does not do.

Data that was exposed by the breach is PHI or Protected Health Information under the HIPAA. According to the Information Security Media Group, the US Department of Health and Human Services has confirmed this is the biggest health data breach since September 2009, when the enforcement of the HIPAA breach notification rule began. Other reports have suggested that the Social Security numbers within the Anthem database were not encrypted.

Analysts have proposed possible theories as to how Anthem attackers could have stolen the password. According to the Associated Press, attackers hijacked the credentials of at least five different employees, with one of them being an administrator at Anthem. The first step the attackers could have taken in their spear-phishing campaign was to gather emails of employees to target. With job postings and profiles of employees available on LinkedIn, this would be trivial for anyone, as several DBAs, system architects and CXOs are to be found there.

The next step in the phishing campaign would be to compromise some high-level employee systems. This would have involved attaching malware to emails or using a browser exploit. Any employee gullible enough to click on the link in their email would have revealed his or her username and password to the attackers who employed sophisticated malware for the purpose. Usually, such attack malware are specifically designed to evade most products that detect anti-virus. Once the credentials are obtained, it is only a matter of time before the actual access to the database begins.

The key weakness here appears to be the lack of any additional authentication mechanism. With a single login using a password or key, attackers had administrative access to the entire database. More than the lack of encryption, Anthem's primary security lapse appears to have been improper access controls. With complete administrative access, even an encrypted database would not have stopped the attackers, unless the policy was specified with the least privileged access rules.

Cloud providers hosting databases do provide several security controls including encryption and data masking abilities. That leaves Anthem's vulnerability to how they had configured their system with access controls based on their operational and business requirements.

RECOMMENDATIONS FOR PROTECTING AGAINST ANTHEM-LIKE ATTACKS

Setting access controls is a troubling issue for several organizations, in which the healthcare industry is not alone. Unless set and implemented rigorously, access controls may increase the risk from phishing and insider threats – mostly from mistakes by users with high-level access. Just as with Anthem, several organizations have loose access controls.

The Anthem incident may have taken longer to detect had the administrator not noticed his own credentials being used to access the database – this could have led to more data being compromised. Obviously, there is a need to monitor the database activity with more regularity.

Compared to other industry sectors such as banking and retail, most healthcare IT infrastructure is not modern and does not meet the current requirements. In addition, technology budgets in healthcare are under the most pressure, simply because the focus is more on the medical aspects rather than IT. This also leads to lower numbers of tech support staff and rising end-of-life equipment without adequate support – increasing the vulnerability of IT systems even more.

With phishing campaigns and similar activities on the rise, it is impossible to keep attackers out. Human fallibility can also not be overruled or overlooked. Therefore, healthcare industry needs to ask that if attackers do enter their systems, what data can they have access to in the organization. With basic frameworks of access controls in place, administrators must evaluate critical security controls with a view to exercising access controls based on the user's need to know.

Regularly monitoring database activity is best left to automated tools rather than to humans. With excellent automated tools available for monitoring enterprise database systems, suspicious activity such as odd-hour access can be easily flagged along with other indicators. Pairing this process with correlation rules from log intelligence tools can enhance the granularity of the monitoring.

Although there is a dire need for increasing the investments for upgrading the aging IT infrastructure in the healthcare systems, this will not happen in the near-term. With the current trend of transitioning from fee-for-service to an outcome-based model, the healthcare sector is seeing reduced reimbursement rates. Although IT investments will continue to nosedive, the healthcare industry must sit up and take note that their IT infrastructure is an important cybersecurity issue while being a patient safety issue at the same time.

CONCLUSION

The healthcare industry would do well to employ Defense-in-Depth strategies while taking advantage of crucial security controls such as Tripwire and Vormetric for protecting their sensitive data.

REFERENCES

Anthem Breach: Phishing Attack Cited

http://www.healthcareinfosecurity.com/anthem-breach-phishing-attack-cited-a-7895

Protecting Against Anthem-Like Attacks

http://www.healthcareinfosecurity.com/protecting-against-anthem-like-attacks-a-7896?rf=2015-02-10-eh&utm_source=SilverpopMailing&utm_medium=email&utm_campaign=enews-his-20150210%20%281%29&utm_content=&spMailingID=7491776&spUserID=NjM5MzgwODg5MDIS1&spJobID=621074881&spReportId=NjIxMDc0ODgxS0

Anthem Offers Services to Breach Victims

http://www.healthcareinfosecurity.com/
anthem-offers-services-to-breach-victims-a-7915

Why The Anthem Breach Just Doesn't Matter Anymore

http://www.forbes.com/sites/quickerbettertech/2015/02/09/
why-the-anthem-breach-just-doesnt-matter-anymore/

What the Anthem Data Breach Says About the Vulnerability of Healthcare IT

http://www.cio.com/article/2880771/data-breach/what-the-anthem-data-breach-says-about-the-vulnerability-of-healthcare-it.html

How Anthem Could Be Breached

http://www.tripwire.com/state-of-security/incident-detection/how-the-anthem-breach-could-have-happened/

ANALYTICS AND DATA MINING IN HEALTHCARE

Statistically speaking, mining of big data and its analytics in healthcare is evolving very fast, while providing insight from extremely large data sets. Although this has huge potential and is already helping to improve outcomes with reduced costs, several challenges still need to be overcome.

Patient care, compliance and regulatory requirements bind the healthcare industry, which has a history of keeping records and in the process, generates a huge amount of data. Traditionally, they store it mostly in hard copy form on paper and film, but the current trend in the healthcare industry is to digitize these massive quantities of data rapidly.

Pressure on the industry to improve its healthcare delivery at reduced costs and comply with mandatory requirements is forcing it to consider the potential of big data, as the vast quantities of data are currently known. The industry is discovering the hidden potential of big data, which includes among others, population health management, disease surveillance and clinical decision support.

A very rudimentary idea of the humongous size comes from reports stating that big data from US healthcare is rapidly approaching the zettabyte scale and will very soon enter the yottabyte. A zettabyte equals 1021GB and one yottabyte is 1024GB. A California-based health network alone is reported to have about 40 petabytes (40x 1,048,576GB) of such data from EHRs.

Common data management tools and traditional methods are woefully inadequate to deal with big data. Even traditional hardware and software finds it difficult to handle the extremely large and complex electronic health data sets that the healthcare industries churn out. Apart from its sheer volume, two aspects make healthcare big data such a daunting prospect – diversity of data types and the speed of handling.

Simply stated, big data in the healthcare industry is made up of information from patient healthcare and well-being. This includes inputs from CPOE and clinical decision support systems, EPRs or electronic patient records, machine generated or sensor data, social media posts and updates, blogs and web pages, data from emergency care, news feeds and articles belonging to medical journals.

Amidst this vast array and amount of data, there is a huge opportunity of discovering associations while understanding the underlying trends and patterns. Big data analytics has the potential to lower costs, save lives and improve health care. The industry can use big data to extract insights leading to better-informed decisions.

New critical factors such as meaningful use and pay for performance are emerging in today's healthcare environment, changing the reimbursement model. Healthcare organizations need to acquire proper tools, infrastructure and techniques for taking effective advantage of big data to prevent potential loss of millions of dollars in revenue and profit.

DATA MINING CHALLENGES IN HEALTHCARE

The $3-trillion US healthcare Industry expects use of big data will improve patient outcomes, make the system more transparent and lead to a more accessible and affordable care. According to the Health Data Consortium, the ability to anticipate and treat illnesses increases manifolds with the power to access and analyze big data. On one hand, this data helps in recognizing individuals at risk related to serious health problems. On the other, it can identify waste in the system as well as lower the cost of healthcare across the board.

Before delivering major insights, companies owning the analytics engines require access to the necessary information. Hospitals, primary care providers, researchers, health insurers, state and federal governments among others hold a staggering amount of healthcare data. The problem – each of these acts as a silo, with only a little transparency across them.

Among the aggregation of massive amounts of data, looms the challenge of maintaining patient privacy. Although the success of big data will not mean private data becomes public, healthcare will have to figure out how to leverage the information for delivering better quality patient care, while keeping the information secure.

A major driving force behind the momentum came from the Affordable Care Act. It incentivized providers to become more data-driven and to facilitate data sharing. Increased sharing will make the entire healthcare system more transparent. For example, big data is proving critical in measuring the success of ACOs or Accountable Care Organizations. However, coordination, collection and analysis of huge amounts of data and implementation of the findings are as yet years down the road.

ANALYTICS AND HEALTH INFORMATICS

Currently, health informatics is entering a new era, where technology is starting to handle big data. This is opening up huge opportunities in data mining and big data analytics helping to realize the goals of diagnosing, treating, helping and healing patients in need. The ultimate goal of this industry is to improve the quality of care that it can provide to end users, that is, improving the domain of HCO or Health Care Output.

Combining computer science and information science within the realm of healthcare produces health informatics. Currently a lot of research is underway within this field including bioinformatics, image informatics, clinical informatics, public health informatics and translational bioinformatics. Research in health informatics covers data acquisition, retrieval, storage and analytics by employing data mining techniques.

Attempts are made to define big data to make it easier to incorporate in various studies. One way of defining big data is by using five V's – Value, Veracity, Variety, Velocity and Volume. While Value defines the quality of data in reference to intended results, Veracity measures how genuine the data is. Where Variety defines the level of complexity, Velocity is the pace at which new data is generated, while Volume points to the physical amount of this data.

Health informatics research uses data that has many of the above stated qualities. Since the basic goal is to improve HCO, most data inherently has high value. Apart from data collected by traditional methods such as in a clinic, which is essentially regarded as being high in value, data gathered from social media may also be regarded as high value.

Data coming from faulty clinical sensors, gene microarray or even from patient information stored in databases may be erroneous, incomplete or noisy. This may be a cause for concern when Health informatics deals with data that requires high veracity. It may be necessary to evaluate such data properly before dealing with it.

Healthcare generates different types of data. For example, search query data may come from different age groups or a complex database. Health informatics has to see this big variety at many levels since there may be a large quantity of varying types of independent attributes.

With new data coming in at increasing speeds, health informatics has to deal with big velocity. Real-time monitoring of events are a common generator for such data, for example, medical sensors tracking or monitoring the current condition of a patient or a multitude of incoming web posts giving the latest situation in an unfolding epidemic.

Big data has huge volumes coming from the large amounts of records hospitals store for patients. Some instances can be quite large, such as when datasets are generated for gene microarray or MRI images for each patient. On the other hand, social media data collected from a large population may also constitute a large pool.

Although defining or classifying big data with the five qualities does not cover all the types encountered by health informatics, most impose significant procedural constraints and require some way of addressing. For example, EHRs may be difficult to store in offline storages because of their high volume, even when not exhibiting big velocity or variety. Real-time continuous data may require very high-throughput processing because of its high velocity, even though it is not big in volume. Big value data without big veracity may require complex methods of adjustment such as expanding the size of the dataset. That means definitions of big data that merely focus on volume and velocity may actually not be considering enough qualities of the dataset to characterize it fully.

Although a lot of research is eventually helping answer events in the clinical realm, in reality, there exists a gap of about 13-17 years between clinical research and actual clinical care hospitals use in practice. Most decisions made these days depend on general information that has worked before. With the explosion of big data and the research in health informatics, healthcare systems will be able to garner new ways of being more accurate, reliable and efficient.

Health informatics gains medical insight from applying analytics and data mining to population data as well. This data may be gathered from experts or hospitals in the traditional form or from social media. Either way, this data has big volume, big velocity and big variety, but possibly low veracity and low value. However, depending on the techniques used for extracting useful information, this type of data may also have big value.

CONCLUSION

Health informatics comprising analytics and data mining in healthcare shows tremendous promise while providing inspiration for the future courses of action. It shows the importance of using all accessible levels of data to advantage. As computational power increases, methods more efficient and accurate will be developed, leading to newer levels of human existence.

REFERENCES

What is Data Mining in Healthcare?
https://www.healthcatalyst.com/data-mining-in-healthcare

A review of data mining using big data in health informatics
http://www.journalofbigdata.com/content/1/1/2

Big data analytics in healthcare: promise and potential
http://www.hissjournal.com/content/2/1/3

How Big Data Will Help Save Healthcare
http://www.forbes.com/sites/castlight/2014/11/10/how-big-data-will-help-save-healthcare/

RISK SHARING BETWEEN HOSPITALS AND OUTSOURCED SERVICES

Healthcare providers are increasingly coming under economic and social pressures that are ultimately affecting their service budgets and the ability to deliver quality services. As with all organizations, healthcare providers also must overcome the tremendous pressures of competition by exploring new managerial approaches to get an edge in the marketplace.

To thrive in this aggressive market, one increasingly attractive approach is outsourcing. While providing an array of broad and complex range of services, hospitals are a particularly fertile environment for outsourcing many of their functions, and they can buy several of these from other institutions.

There are several advantages in providing services with the internal staff. The major advantage is price, assuming that the service levels are equivalent. Other two reasons for retaining services with the internal staff are continuity and vested interests.

As internal staff has been with the hospital for a longer time, they have a better understanding of the patients' requirements and strategies to be followed, such as in an emergency. Added to this is the anticipation of continuity – they will be available to deal with the consequences of their actions. That leads to better strategic alignment through improved relationships, paying off in greater client satisfaction.

Although the use of internal staff has advantages, outsourcing also offers several unique benefits.

ADVANTAGES OF OUTSOURCING SERVICES

With increasing volume of service, unit costs tend to go down. In such situations, outsourcing can save money through economies of scale. Individual hospitals may be unable to match the level of expenses achieved by external service providers as they combine their volumes of service to multiple healthcare units.

For example, the pharmaceutical industry relies on outsourcing to handle clinical trials of experimental drugs for them. Clinical trials need the right medical investigators such as doctors and medical researchers, along with healthy patients willing to submit themselves to experimentation. The outsourcing industry spends a significant amount of time and money for developing relationships with hospitals and clinicians that offer patients for such trials – an activity that cannot be economically taken up by the pharmaceutical companies by themselves.

However, saving money through outsourcing is possible only when three conditions are satisfied – there are economies of scale, the economies are accessible across corporate boundaries and the savings are sufficient to generate profit even after paying off all stakeholders.

As with other industries, healthcare cannot invest all its eggs in one basket and must offer diverse services. Doing this spreads the risk, while the hospital reduces its total risk. By outsourcing some services, hospitals can further reduce their risk by sharing it with the service provider. One way such outsourcing helps is by minimizing the fluctuations resulting from peaks and valleys in demand.

For example, for handling sudden peaks in healthcare, such as during a sudden outbreak of flu, a hospital may have to hire additional staff likely to become surplus once the outbreak contains itself. Outsourcing by hiring contractors at per-hour expense is one way of handling this situation. However, the expense of hiring additional staff and retaining them should offset the added expenses of outsourcing. If there are frequent peak loads with short valleys, hiring may prove more economic rather than outsourcing. For occasional peaks, contractors will save money even if they charge higher by the hour.

Hospitals can develop internal staff by outsourcing some of their routine, less interesting and end-of-life work, leaving staff free to engage in new and developmental opportunities. On the other hand, the reverse might prove detrimental to the hospital's business endeavors. Increasing dependence on the vendor, while leaving the internal staff to deal with obsolescent work, might send signals to the staff that the hospital is disinterested in investing in their professional growth.

To some extent, hospitals can engage consultants in staff augmentation. This is especially useful in situations where it is necessary for the hospital to allow external consultants transfer their methods and skills to improve the effectiveness of internal employees. They work together on real projects, while teaching the staff and the benefits are lasting.

The current need for outsourcing stems from the need to be proactive. Hospitals are almost always very close to the edge – mostly due to thinning margins, increasing patient expectations and scant help from the government. However, most hospitals now understand the perils of focusing on short-term, tactical solutions to immediate issues and problems. They recognize that the key to survival lies in leveraging the organizational strengths while making continuous incremental improvements in their effectiveness and efficiency – more often than not by using outside service providers.

CONCERNS WITH OUTSOURCING SERVICES

The main concern with outsourcing services lies in the way hospitals use their electronic healthcare records. Privacy concerns might prevent healthcare companies in outsourcing software development and records management. Other concerns with outsourcing may be legal and regulatory issues.

There are several ancillary services in hospitals where outsourcing can be a boon for both. Such partnerships allow the hospital and the vendor to do what they do best. While the ancillary service providers bring in capital and management expertise, the hospital can focus on inpatient care. However, such deals can be rather complex. Parties to such arrangements should be experienced in balancing business objectives against the laws, rules and regulations of the land. In addition, there may also be specific concerns affecting the decision to outsource.

Assuming that a service provider is not a part of the organization, they may not show much interest in long-term strategic considerations. This could lead to a loss of mission, as the long-term partner may prefer to get on board with the strategic mission of the organization.

Loss of control may easily arise in long-term relationships unless the hospital ensures its retention. The hospital must actively manage the outsourcing relationship, by conducting regular reviews while insisting on improving service quality.

Although organizations do not outsource for innovations, but for performance of current service-delivery capabilities, there can be a concern about sacrificing long-term value and innovation. In reality, outsourcing tactical activities frees organizational employees to pursue long-term planning and innovation.

There may be concern about performance issues, as the perception of outside vendors is that they have inadequate skills compared to internal staff. Such concerns may turn out baseless, as hospitals engage service providers in long-term relationships with their patients.

Cultural barriers may pose significant problems on multiple levels. External personnel may not have the same commitment to patient satisfaction, to deadlines, to cost containment and quality that internal staff has. This may prove to be an impediment to an organization achieving a good working relationship with the external agency. Organizations may succeed here by setting up basic guidelines for use and by creating an internal group for overseeing the relationship.

As each institution is different, complex healthcare environments require unique processes for developing and implementing organizational changes. Although a basic set of characteristics may be commonly applicable to all institutions, to meet specific outcomes for an institute requires sophisticated change initiatives and processes designed specifically for those outcomes.

THE VALUES HEALTHCARE MUST BE LOOKING AT FROM OUTSOURCING

The healthcare organization must have some metrics to assess the value of its increased commitment from outsourcing its services at comprehensive and strategic levels. Some key tests the organization may use are:

Impact to Employee Satisfaction: Is internal staff experiencing greater job satisfaction with being able to invest more of their time in being strategic and innovative because of outsourced functions?

Impact to Patient Satisfaction: Is the outside provider able to deliver the same or better quality of service to patients as compared to that delivered by in-house personnel? Is the hospital staff now more attentive to the core functions because of outsourcing to outside service providers?

Adding To the Economic Value: Is the other party more efficient in delivering services that allows the healthcare services to achieve cost savings? Is the health institute able to avoid costs by offloading its functions?

Competitive Advantages Gained: Is the facility better able to compete because of outsourcing? Are prospective and existing clients increasing their service arrangements with the institution because of outsourced services?

Allocation of Resources: Is the outsourced service provider delivering and continue to deliver the required quality of service and scope through committed human resources, technology, expertise and capital? Is the agreed objective of the relationship being appropriately honored by the current allocation of resources and is the division mutually satisfactory?

CONCLUSION

Customer expectations are growing and so are the costs and the competition. On the other hand, healthcare institutes face an ever-changing environment, where the profits tend to nosedive, capacity is driven down and the levels of service keep shrinking. In this bleak scenario, the benefits of outsourcing non-medical services can be a viable strategy for hospitals.

To sum up the advantages of outsourcing, hospitals can expect access to capital improvement dollars, risk sharing, improved cost avoidance and savings, greater access to resources, better employee retention and increased patient satisfaction.

Long-term strategic partnerships with outsourcing providers may also introduce healthcare organizations to market opportunities beyond their core competence. A smaller number of long-term outside service providers with a strategic partnership may prove to be a more comprehensive arrangement as compared to large numbers of single-purpose, short-term, ad-hoc outsourcing relationships.

REFERENCES

Essential Link of Non-Clinical Services to Quality Care

http://www.google.co.in/url?sa=t&rct=j&q=&esrc=s&source=web&cd=1&ved=0CB8QFjAA&url=http%3A%2F%2Fwww.aramark.com%2FWorkArea%2FDownloadAsset.aspx%3Fid%3D425&ei=PyDjVNmcFIa3uATeiIKQCw&usg=AFQjCNEqMmS9xcBRXbyxGFwgYM68uR8xNA&sig2=9gxcagF3v7HZUxPgct8EbA&bvm=bv.85970519,d.c2E

Outsourcing Ambulatory and Outpatient Services: What Hospitals Need to Know

http://www.healthcarelawtoday.com/2014/10/29/outsourcing-ambulatory-and-outpatient-services-what-hospitals-need-to-know/

IT Outsourcing in US Hospitals: Potential Benefits and Risks

http://citeseerx.ist.psu.edu/viewdoc/download?doi=10.1.1.200.5433&rep=rep1&type=pdf

EHR Outsourcing Challenged By Privacy & Efficiency Concerns

http://www.cmswire.com/cms/information-management/ehr-outsourcing-challenged-by-privacy-efficiency-concerns-009084.php

RISKS INVOLVED WITH UNPROTECTED DIGITAL HEALTHCARE DATA

Increased demand for data from patients and proliferation of mobile devices has severely increased the security concerns of healthcare providers. Additionally, providers now must primarily ensure that they are meeting the HIPAA compliance and patient data security as they expand their security coverage to protect employees, most of whom use mobile and other devices such as remote printers.

Healthcare organizations are required to update their legacy software periodically to stay ahead of newer security threats and avoid theft and breach of patient data. Moreover, they need to do this without restricting access to data and services.

According to the latest California Data Breach Report, data breaches in healthcare are increasing at 28%. Of this, more than 70% of the personal records compromised were because of lost or stolen unencrypted portable devices such as laptops. The report recommends encryption as an absolute necessity for the healthcare industry, applicable to all computers in offices, including mobile and portable media.

Digital healthcare data such as PHI must be protected, since health information often has to be shared externally with providers, insurers and other third parties who, in turn, can forward it to other parties. Added to this is the threat from cyber-attacks, which makes encryption a key tool for keeping highly sensitive data safe as required under HIPAA.

RISK VS. EFFICIENCY OF EMERGING CLOUD TECHNOLOGIES

Although businesses still have mixed feelings about emerging cloud technologies, this cannot be ignored where healthcare security is concerned. Apart from fulfilling security needs, cloud technology also brings in greater efficiency to the healthcare business. According to a study by Insights, a provider of SaaS technology, although the promise of improved efficiency is leading businesses towards adopting the cloud technology, not many have a very deep trust in the security provided by clouds.

According to the Insight report, most businesses that adopted cloud services were in it mainly for the money saved due to the minimizing of infrastructure costs and reduced reliance on internal IT functions. However, apart from making things cheaper, the cloud technology is also making things better for businesses.

Current advances have mitigated the risks of security associated earlier with cloud technology. This has made it not only a more secure option, but also cheaper. Therefore, healthcare enterprises and organizations can now do more with less.

This shift in data storage and transportation to clouds, including several data breaches in the industry, has led to an increased focus on data security. Healthcare organizations find that they have to deal with growing cyber-attacks mainly on their unprotected data floating around in the clouds. According to the IDC report, by 2020, healthcare will be passing 80% of their data through clouds with about 42% of it unprotected. Therefore, it can be concluded that there will be a tremendous increase in the amount of unprotected data leading to more data breaches, unless something is done about it.

GUARDING SECURE DATA

With the commencement of the omnibus rule, every IT executive is making it his or her top priority to secure patient data and comply with HIPAA requirements. Additionally, CISOs and CIOs are constantly evaluating the best way to monitor and ensure the protection of patient data. This assumes importance given the constant changes and additions the health IT infrastructure and systems are subject to, along with the increasing threats from the cyber-crime world.

Commonly used PC products nearing their end-of-life cycles and no longer receiving vendor security updates and patches pose a looming risk to data security. Apart from PCs, hospital facilities use several other products, such as workstations, applications, routers, hypervisors and medical devices. All of them require vendor support to be maintained with the latest firmware, fixes or stable updates. Additionally, several devices will not run on the latest versions of the Operating Systems.

Ensuring patient data security generally requires workstations and other devices are patched and updated with the latest products from third-party vendors. IT staffers need to maintain a database apart from using suitable software programs to track all the relevant applications and devices posing a security risk.

When periodically reviewed, the records will be used more as points of reference. When the vendors inform regarding security updates and fixes, the records can be referenced to see what upgrades and actions are required to ensure continued compliance to HIPAA.

Some vulnerability can be expected with legacy systems in use within hospitals. Although attackers may never exploit all the existing vulnerabilities, it is necessary to understand the risks involved with and the precautions required in safeguarding electronic health records. Being fully aware of the risks associated with each product bring used is critical to managing PHI.

When keeping track of updates and versions from vendors, it will be obvious that some vendors are more prompt than others in issuing frequent releases of security patches. Future system upgrades and purchase decisions can be based on such information for minimizing data security risk.

PERFORMING RISK ASSESSMENTS IN HEALTH IT ENVIRONMENTS

Building a solid EHR or electronic health record security ecosystem is a constant challenge that health IT owners regularly face. Creating a strong information security program for health IT owners begins with an assessment of security risks. That not only allows the organization to make informed decisions related to security, it also offers the organization an insight into the security postures adopted within its walls and outside.

Many health IT owners prefer to focus on securing data within their data centers. That is because most CIOs, CMIOs and even CSIOs do not clearly focus on or understand the threats and issues existing outside their data centers. They need to focus on measures necessary to tackle data breaches, hacker attacks and theft. These and other external factors require adequate personnel, processes and technologies.

Securing healthcare organizations starts with a vision from the health IT owners. Unless they can properly enumerate all the processes, technologies and stakeholders along with the associated risk, they will find it almost impossible to design and implement suitable controls.

Any small to mid-sized healthcare organization can have a population numbering in hundreds if not in thousands. Factor in the number of technologies and processes that this population works with, and it is easy to see that the situation is overwhelming. Only when a clear vision is established, can there be easier design, control and implementation, along with proper decision-making related to information security. Additionally, vision clarity also leads to a significant decrease in the risks to protected information assets.

It is necessary to conduct a security risk assessment review for all existing controls – physical, technical and administrative – both within and outside the organization. These controls can be analyzed against frameworks of best practices and the risks and gaps quantified for creating a program roadmap.

Following a proper review, the outcome will generate a comprehensive assessment of the organization's security program, a set of recommendations and a clear roadmap along with a remediation plan.

A proper assessment will ensure that the organization will be secure from inside as well as out, it will align business and compliance drivers and will provide a critical view of the current position of the organization's security. Furthermore, risk assessment is necessary for satisfying meaningful use criteria when receiving federal incentives.

STEPS FOR SECURITY RISK ASSESSMENTS

Discover drivers and objectives – Identify the drivers and objectives early on to make sure the results of security risk assessment are tailored to fit the organization. Those most important could be operational drivers, business objectives, regulatory drivers, staffing and fiscal responsibility.

The discovery phase brings forth all the information and documentation related to people, process and technology. It is very important that the person actually doing the assessment understands the processes and lifecycle of the information used by the data owners and or other stakeholders.

Being the longest phase in the process of risk assessment, discovery ensures that all information is collected and all processes are acknowledged and understood. This is a vital phase providing the necessary groundwork for a solid risk assessment offering optimal value.

Assess, analyze and quantify – Use a framework to assess, analyze and quantify all the information collected in the earlier phase. Several regulatory drivers author best practices frameworks. References are the ISO or International Standards Organization, NIST or National Institute of Standards and Technology and ISACA or the Information Systems Audit and Control Association.

By following a simple arrangement, applicable regulatory drivers can be mapped to the chosen best practices framework. This makes monitoring and reporting regulatory compliance almost painless. Comparing the collected information against control statements or objectives within the chosen framework quantifies the current state of the security position of the organization and its pertinent compliance status.

Recommendations for gaps and weaknesses – The output of the previous assessment phase will be a bulleted list of the good, the bad and the ugly of the security position of the organization. The recommendations phase must align any gaps and weaknesses with the objectives and drivers identified in the discovery phase. That will generate the necessary recommendations to close the gaps and strengthen the weaknesses.

Phase all recommendations to categories such as tactical, mid-term and strategic. For example, the tactical period could be six to eight weeks; the mid-term could be for two to six months, while the strategic period could range from six to 20 months. This allows for implementing quick-fixes and low-effort remediation immediately, while longer-term processes that involve re-engineering processes and purchasing technologies are planned properly involving all the stakeholders.

Review all recommendations – Review all recommendations with stakeholders and business units for ensuring their suitability and alignment with the business operations and vision.

CONCLUSION

With a well-planned security risk assessment, stakeholders have the vision and information for taking key decisions. That ensures the proper protection of critical information assets. Additionally, it allows the strategic security program to evolve with updated legislation and standards, emerging technologies and organizational goals.

REFERENCES

California Data Breach Report Says Encryption for Healthcare is a Must

http://blog.hisoftware.com/2014/privacy/california-data-breach-report-says-encryption-for-healthcare-is-a-must

Predicting Health IT Needs in 2015: Scratching the Data Security Itch

http://etherfax.net/predicting-health-needs-2015-scratching-data-security-itch/

How to perform a security risk assessment in a health IT environment

http://searchhealthit.techtarget.com/tip/How-to-perform-a-security-risk-assessment-in-a-health-IT-environment

UNDERSTANDING INFORMATION SYSTEMS ARCHITECTURE

Any business or organization needs an overall structure to operate effectively and efficiently. Proper communication and information flow form the underlying foundation of this structure. The organization must formally define its business processes and rules, technical framework, systems structure and product technologies – through its information systems architecture. Typically, the information systems architecture consists of four layers – business processes, systems architecture, technical expertise and processes and product delivery.

Solutions reach the final consumer of services via the hardware and software that the organization uses. The architecture of the business' information system encompasses the internal processes and delivery methods. Mainly, the architecture describes the design and contents of a computerized system. Once documented, the architecture provides information on the detailed inventory of current hardware, software and networking capabilities. It also encompasses long-range plans, priorities for future purchases and a plan for upgrading and or replacing dated software and equipment. In general, the information system architecture should document:

- The type of data/information stored
- Methods and processes of system functions
- Location of different components
- Timing and occurrences of activities and events in the system
- Reasons for existence of the system

One of the most urgent priorities of the healthcare information systems is the integration and evolution of their existing systems. They need to do this to allow the entire organization meet the increasing clinical, managerial and organizational needs. An open architecture may be founded on the initiation of a middleware of common healthcare-specific services. On one hand, this reduces the efforts necessary for allowing existing systems to interwork. On the other, it also automatically establishes a functional and information basis common to the entire organization. Newer applications may then be allowed to develop rapidly on top of this system while natively integrating with the rest of the system. The Standard Architecture for Healthcare Information Systems CEN/TC251/PT1-013 defines such systems formalized through the proposed European preStandard.

Several hospitals and healthcare industries are already demonstrating the validity and effectiveness of the practicality of this approach with the utilization of the DHE middleware. Healthcare, being an information intensive industry, requires reliable and timely information as a critical resource for planning and monitoring service provisions at all levels of functioning and analysis.

That has made ICT or Information and Communication Technologies indispensable in the healthcare sector. General perception is health care needs to pull itself up by its shoestrings very fast, as it is ten years behind in use of ICT as compared to other industrial sectors such as banking, airlines and manufacturing industries. However, this perception is changing rapidly.

ADOPTION OF INFORMATION AND COMMUNICATION TECHNOLOGIES IN HEALTH CARE

Health care has been adopting ICT through a series of evolving phases. Financial systems were the first to adopt health informatics - they provided support to the billing payroll, accounting and reporting systems of organizations. Later, clinical departments took up the initiative to support internal activities such as laboratory, radiology and pharmacy, mostly as machinery and standardized procedures evolved to support high-volume operations.

When health care made major investments in cost accounting and materials management systems, ICT once again gained prominence in financial systems. Lately, attention is turning towards enterprise-wide clinical systems, including clinical data repositories and EHRs or Electronic Health Records.

Health care organizations, under the pressures of technology-pushing forces, initially tended to adopt these ICT-based solutions uncritically. Their ICT adoption had limited analysis of the organizational consequences, with only a modest focus on both the improvement of effectiveness as well as the support of the core care processes. These factors led to a historically low level of emphasis on ICT governance determined by an inhomogeneous development of HCISs or Health Care Information Systems.

Recent years have seen health care providers face an unprecedented era of pressures and competition to improve the effectiveness and quality of care. That is leading to changes in the behavior of modeling techniques involving innovative information Systems. Health care is exploring comprehensive perspectives to allow ICT to improve the quality of managerial processes leading to improvements in quality of care, while simultaneously reducing their costs.

HEALTH CARE INFORMATION SYSTEMS

Under current perspectives, HCISs are made up of different systems, orchestrated and integrated to support care in a patient-centric view of processes and procedures in the organization. Therefore, HCISs offer a tremendous support for cost management in the healthcare sector and for improving the quality of care. With the introduction of HCISs, healthcare organizations are now able to capture, store, process and communicate information timely to decision makers. This leads to a better coordination of health care at all levels of analysis.

When compared to the traditional streams of research on information systems, HCIS has not only flourished, but has also germinated a variety of emerging theoretical frameworks, empirical research and practitioner-based literature. Therefore, HCIS can be defined as a powerful ICT-based tool to improve the effectiveness and efficiency of the health care delivery by providing a synergy of three disciplines – health care management, organization management and information management. Additionally, HCISs also amalgamate various other applications that support the needs of the health care sector, such as clinicians, patients and policy makers. Using HCIS makes it simpler to collect and manage all data related to both the administrative and clinical processes in health care.

While a number of systems can use this data, the most effective use comes from integrating it with data form several other entities. This is especially true for patient data, which must be subject to very strict rules in terms of both security safeguards as well as confidentiality.

ELEMENTS THAT MAKE HCISS SO SPECIFIC

Compared to information systems in other industries, HCISs are specific to the healthcare industry. The distinctiveness that characterizes the development of HCIS in health care can be attributed to six elements.

Information mismatch – At all stages related to care, information systems can highlight and monitor errors, since the quality of health care is vigilantly executed and diligently pursued to reduce the gravity associated with information mismatch.

The personal nature of information – Health information systems mostly manage information of personal nature. Most of the data transfer between different health care entities involves actual and perceived risk of information falling into the wrong hands. This perception of compromised privacy makes each information exchange in the health domain becomes extremely complex.

The influence of regulators and competition – All patient data in the healthcare sector is subject to regulatory policies. Providers of ICT-based solutions experience additional difficulties when organizations exploit the advantages of their offers. That makes it more complex for realizing ICT-driven innovations within the health care industry.

Hierarchy and professionalism – Powerful actors such as the hierarchical nature and professionals driving the health care organizations often resist technology, creating barriers to fully exploiting all the potentials associated with health information systems.

Multidisciplinary actors – Although ICT faces multiple barriers in health care, there is an overall unity in the use of HCISs. This is because of most of the health care services are interdisciplinary in nature. This heterogeneity of disciplines in health care makes using ICT very complex – forcing an approach that makes the information system different from the simple classification system usually followed in other industries.

Implementation, learning and adaptation – Within health care delivery, there is a perpetual tension between the need for orderly routines on one hand and on the other, there is a need for sensitivity to changes in local conditions. Because of this tension, the importance of effective learning and adaptation surrounding the implementation of HCISs increases many folds. The acuteness of the situation can be estimated from the fact that solutions that work well in one specific context in health care do not necessarily work in others.

INFORMATION SYSTEMS AND THEIR ARCHITECTURE

System development and enterprise architecture effectively define the broad structure of a system. This may consist of different parts with interrelationships and other properties. When the constituent units such as the business architecture, information system architecture and the technological architecture come together, they ensure that the organization is able to:

- Justify stakeholder requirements
- Fit IT to business purposes
- Harmonize all departments
- Advance and elevate security
- Generate consistency and data integrity
- Become cost-effective by reducing duplication

However, merely enunciation of the architecture tasks will not be enough for the organization. Only a proper engagement process can successful put these objectives into practice. Apart from helping to establish the different ways in which the architecture process can be managed, this also helps to establish the rules of governance.

CONCLUSION

Information systems in health care are processes that involve all key stakeholders in the company's IT and business goals. This includes the project management team, business unit management and the company's overall management. This entails transparent decision-making in the governance process of the enterprise architecture ensuring that organizational changes move in the desired direction, while simultaneously implementing objectives and goals. Such governance processes may include enforced or clearly spelled rules or they may also be IT principles broadly defined. Apart from allowing and organization to achieve its IT visions, Information systems clearly help in creating and enforcing accountability.

REFERENCES

Enterprise architecture and system development

http://www.eacoe.org/information-systems-architecture.php

Enterprise Modelling and Information Systems Architectures - An International Journal

http://www.wi-inf.uni-duisburg-essen.de/MobisPortal/index.php?&groupId=1&&contentType=Profile

Information System Architecture

http://dssresources.com/glossary/116.php

What is information architecture?

http://www.steptwo.com.au/papers/kmc_whatisinfoarch/

Healthcare information systems architecture.

http://www.ncbi.nlm.nih.gov/pubmed/10175347

THE DIGITAL DILEMMA OF HEALTH INFORMATION EXCHANGE

Stakeholders of US healthcare organizations share health information among themselves, within defined geographic areas. Entities such as the HIEs or Health Information Exchanges usually govern such electronic sharing for improving health and care within the community. Creation of HIEs follows the fundamental concept that exchanging health information electronically is instrumental in improving the delivery of care in the US.

HIEs vary widely in their scope, form, structure and content. For example, varying governance and geographic scope allows some HIEs to serve only a state or a small region geographically, while others can serve multi-state regions. Their technical models also differ, with some acting as repositories of health data with others serving as conduits of health information. The services offered and the types of clinical data exchanged by HIEs vary widely as well.

POTENTIAL ADVANTAGES FROM HIES

Healthcare organizations participating in HIEs can expect several potential gains in efficiency and quality in care. However, participants such as physicians must study an HIE thoroughly for identifying any potential disadvantages before they sign a contract. Major topics of concern with HIE participation can be related to negative impact on the work flow of physicians, HIPAA compliance with data security and privacy requirements, unique liability situations, use of HIE data for purposes unrelated to treatment, costs and risks.

Recently, several HIEs were dissolved. This has raised additional concerns regarding the sustainability and viability of HIEs. Physicians investing in technology upgrades and work flow changes to participate in HIEs could see their investments wasted if the HIE were to collapse. These and above issues emphasize that physicians must thoroughly understand the implications of joining the HIE before they make a final decision.

Each individual HIE will offer different services. However, most of them offer common functionalities as initiatives for joining. These functionalities include clinical decision support tools, health summaries for continuity of care, connectivity to EHRs or electronic health records, and many more.

Group practices and physicians joining an HIE will see many potential benefits. This includes advantages in sending and receiving information. A physician or a group's operation benefits in many ways with the HIE providing inbound and outbound data. This includes minimized service duplication, reduced health care costs, availability of information when and where needed, improved safety and quality of patient care, and many more.

FINANCIAL COSTS OF HIES

Physicians participating in specific HIEs should carefully investigate the direct and indirect costs involved, as the cost of participation is dependent upon specific initiatives. The direct costs of participation is the fees associated with accessing HIE data, with the fees being charged depending on the specific HIE as per annum, per month, per transaction or a combination of subscription and transaction fees. In case the HIE is initially dependent upon federal funds, over time, there may be changes in the participation fees charged. Physicians should be careful about future price changes and their notifications.

HIE participation may also include additional expenses of upgrading the office IT systems that physicians use. This may be necessary to meet the system requirements of the HIE. Additionally, changes in workflow processes during the implementation phase will lead to lost revenue and productivity – the indirect costs. The direct and indirect costs will determine the overall cost of participation and this must be factored in before making a final decision regarding an HIE.

POTENTIAL LIABILITY CONCERNS INVOLVING HIES

HIE participation involves potential liabilities, both primary and secondary, and physicians must understand how these liabilities will be shared among the participants. Potential liability concerns involving HIEs include those related to data storage and management, data accuracy and completeness, decisions made with inaccurate data, reproducibility of data at any particular moment, duty to review and availability of access and audit logs. Physicians must note that HIE liability is still evolving and this field generally lacks legal precedent.

HEALTH INFORMATION EXCHANGES IN PRACTICE

One of the major issues for both patients and their physicians is accessing the data within HIEs. By exchanging clinical data among healthcare organizations, physicians gain the opportunity of improving care coordination and quality of care, while minimizing duplication of services and reducing costs. Additionally, physicians are concerned that HIE data could also be used to profile them or evaluate their performance.

Physicians must establish in detail who can access what data within the HIE, and how they will use the information. This is critical before signing an agreement to participate in an HIE, as data access and use varies considerably within HIEs.

HIPAA does not cover HIEs as entities. Rather, they are considered as business associates of entities covered under HIPAA. Therefore, participating covered entities, including physicians, must enter contracts or other agreements with an HIE. The agreement must be as a business associate, to appropriately protect and safeguard the privacy of protected health information. Therefore, whatever system the HIE may be using, it must comply with the privacy and security provisions of HIPAA. Before participating in an HIE, physicians should seek clarification about the potential HIE partner's security and privacy safeguards; they should also ask about how the HIE will be managing data breaches.

HOW EASY IS IT TO SUSTAIN HEALTH INFORMATION EXCHANGES?

Health information exchange is instrumental in the overall effort to build an interconnected delivery system for health care. HIEs have a tremendous potential to improve the quality of health care, reduce medical errors while lowering costs by increasing interoperability and information sharing among payers, providers, patients and other stakeholders.

The HIE workgroup of the HIT Policy Committee is focusing on building healthcare provider directories to facilitate data exchanges. They have described the technical aspects of information exchange in three necessary components when healthcare data is transported from point A to point B. According to the work group, the three necessary components are -

- A routing method (for example, SMPT, SOAP, REST)
- A directory to tell where to route

- A certificate management for ensuring the message is not read or modified during transmission.

If connections were all point-to-point, getting a message from point A to point B could be very messy. That means if health information exchange is to take place, each practice would need to connect separately to all the data sources individually – leading to a practically impossible situation. HIE, which fundamentally acts as a data-exchange clearinghouse, is the solution working to address this dilemma.

This clearinghouse acts rather like a hub, allowing subscribers to route information to its connections. Such clearinghouses are abundant, a good example being the billing world, where a billing program sends all claims to a central hub, which, after making sure of the proper format, forwards the bills to the final recipients.

However, the actual dilemma of HIEs is not in the technical aspects of the exchange. The real question that comes across is: with a system of HIEs across the country, how are these organizations expected to sustain themselves moving forward? There are other concerns as well, such as what business models will they use? Will physicians have to pay a fee to get records from local hospitals? Rather than policy and technical issues, these and similar questions will likely have a greater impact on the evolution of health data exchange.

Different HIE models have emerged and are emerging in this era of ARRA and HITECH. Among them, the most successful model so far has been the one that levies a transaction fees along with a subscription. This model is very similar to the billing-service clearinghouse model.

HIE funding has a potentially significant role for the health insurance plans or payers, who find immediate political advantages in providing funds to help develop and operate HIEs. When such organizations take a larger role in paying for such networks, the largest financial benefit accrues to them and payers gain much more than just good will.

With HIEs lowering the costs by identifying diseases earlier and reducing duplicate tests, payers can invest in strategies that create long-term loyalties among patients and plan providers. In addition, with a fully functioning HIE, payers gain an opportunity of creating financial incentives for participating hospitals and physicians. This could include cost reductions such as discounts on fees.

Much attention has been paid to aspects such as ensuring security and privacy of the data being transmitted. Currently, seed money for launching HIEs is part of HITECH. Once the initial funding runs out, HIE sustainability in these organizations will depend on the business models they follow.

Although the most effective means to achieve sustainability for many HIEs is currently the membership-subscription model enhanced by transaction fees, what is still uncertain is who pays these fees. This context demands a more prominent role of payers or health plans.

CONCLUSION

While most institutions are willing to invest in complex, expensive and large EHR or Electronic Health Record systems, individual physicians are either unable to or unwilling to do so. However, when introduced to free, web-based options, the uptake from physicians was staggering. This is not surprising, given that physicians bear much of the workload brunt of a changeover to digitization, but receive little immediate financial benefit. Therefore, there is every reason to believe physicians are enthusiastic about using HIEs to access outside medical data and get that information into their charts by paying a subscription.

REFERENCES

Sharing Patient Records Is Still A Digital Dilemma For Doctors
http://www.npr.org/blogs/health/2015/03/06/388999602/sharing-patient-records-is-still-a-digital-dilemma-for-doctors

Health Information Exchange (HIE)
http://www.himss.org/library/health-information-exchange

Health Information Exchanges
http://www.ama-assn.org/ama/pub/advocacy/topics/digital-health/health-information-exchanges.page

THIRD PLATFORM TECHNOLOGIES IN HEALTHCARE

The IT industry started with first platform behemoths such as the mainframes, which later gave way to the second platform, the client/servers that came into prominence with the proliferation of desktop computers. Currently, the IT industry is thriving on the third platform of computing, namely, cloud computing, mobiles, big data and the social networks. This is a much bigger influencer of the IT world as compared to the first and second platforms ever were. Not only the IT industry, anyone doing business in today's world is affected, and that includes the healthcare industry as well.

Therefore, very little additional investment is going towards the legacy IT infrastructure – the first and second platforms. While the major investments are moving towards the third platform, industry is utilizing some of this investment to rip out the existing legacy environment and replacing it with SaaS or Software as a Service.

While the strategic issue for enterprise IT users is how to quickly reorient their budgets, for third-platform providers, the issue is how to quickly meet the critical demands of enterprise IT in identifying, selecting, learning and implementing new platforms. For both, rapid reskilling is an urgent necessity – leading to a huge employee churn as everyone adjusts to the reality of this new infrastructure.

THE STRONGLY GROWING PUBLIC CLOUD

According to IDC, the private vs. public cloud computing war is decisively leaning towards public cloud computing. IDC predicts that the share of public CSPs or Could Service Providers will be a full 75% of the total investment in cloud use in the near future and increase thereafter.

The imbalance between the spending on private and public growth has occurred due to the massive growth in the demand for public cloud adoption. Not many are willing to spend on internal private environments, given that operating with public cloud is getting more secure and less expensive. According to IDC, this imbalance is going to be even more pronounced in 2015 and beyond.

This dramatic shift towards public cloud computing is affecting the server market as well. A majority of server shipments, including those from ODMs, is going towards datacenters of cloud service providers, and this is expected to grow further. This also means that server companies are increasingly focusing their new designs on the requirements of CSPs.

OFFERING HEALTHCARE IT AS A SERVICE

According to a joint report from MeriTalk and EMC, healthcare providers will save money in the long run by adopting cloud technology, analytics, mobile and social media. They could even use their EHR systems as a service. This is likely to happen soon, as IT leaders try to bring the SMAC stack or Social, Mobile, Analytics and Cloud technology together into a single, integrated architecture.

With this type of architecture, healthcare can easily catch up to other verticals in the industry. With SMAC, hospitals can demonstrate a return on investment in EHR or electronic health record systems. Moving beyond meaningful use, hospitals can offer IT as a service leveraging it both within and outside its walls.

Healthcare providers are increasingly turning towards SMAC stack, referring to the collective technology or the third platform as Futurecare. For example, many ambulatory providers are increasingly using cloud EHR; increased use of common analytics is reducing risk analysis and readmissions; providers are increasingly using mobile health to view patient information, receiving clinical information and filling electronic prescriptions; social technology is increasingly helping to improve communication among physicians and with patients.

Each type of technology component within the SMAC stack supports a different step in the management of population health. For example, the use of cloud offers access, use of big data offers identification, using mobility enables engagement between physicians and patients, while social technology triggers perpetual activation. This is one way healthcare CIOs should think of their EHR systems – as providing IT as a service. This will allow them to exhibit ROI even after meeting meaningful use.

THE THIRD PLATFORM AND INFORMATION TO PATIENTS

Since the passage of healthcare reform legislation in 2010, the implementation of electronic records and technologies and the offer of incentives from the government for meaningful uses or IT, the healthcare industry in the US are currently going through a rapid transformation. A greater collaboration between providers and payers can be expected as these changes reflect increasingly in business models. The erstwhile fee-for-service model is slowly giving way to fee-for-value incentives.

The third platform and its components, SMAC, are playing a decisive role in this alteration. Healthcare is taking advantage of cloud-based portals using industry-specific solutions. Analytics and mobile solutions are proving effective in removing surprises from the process, and for tightening patient engagement. Healthcare as a whole is moving towards a goal of reducing costs, while simultaneously improving the quality of care and outcomes.

If there are sudden health issues, such as accidents and emergencies including serious ones, the present healthcare industry can take care very well. It has also done wonders in the field of public health. However, healthcare faces the maximum cost challenge when treating chronic conditions. This is mostly related to the aging population that is living longer.

With inappropriate technology, it becomes an expensive and difficult proposition to treat the previously mentioned conditions. However, with solutions from the third platform, things are changing for the better.

In the US, some mobile service providers are pursuing an innovative initiative wherein they offer customers advertising services with greater personalization and relevance. Such offers in the third platform can engage patients by offering them information helping them to make the best choice about key health-related decisions.

Healthcare providers are increasingly using predictive analytics supported by cloud, social, mobile and big data services to use education, social influence and even sending reminders to patients, thereby helping to change their behavior.

Healthcare providers have always found providing individualized care to be an expensive proposition. This was mostly because their staff had to manage the regime of each patient individually. With the third platform technologies, the process can be automated and made cost-effective. Moreover, proactive care, such as prenatal information services, can be easily provided with regimens tailored to the needs of the individual. Today, most healthcare systems and private payers are trying to manage the health of the population by experimenting with these technologies.

WHAT HEALTHCARE SHOULD LOOK FOR WHEN IMPLEMENTING THIRD PLATFORM

According to IDC, there are some important factors to be taken care of when the healthcare industry takes the initiative of using third platform solutions. These new digital transformation initiatives may also be considered as best practices.

Refreshing Competence In IT – Third platform solutions require skills significantly different from what was necessary for first and second platforms. Social technologies, mobile, big data and cloud require a fresh look at the new technologies and business practices. Healthcare needs to focus more on their core competence by becoming leaner and outsourcing more of their non-core activities.

Rethinking The Basic Business Model – The third platform takes the existing business model and stands it on its head. Not only does it touch upon the organizational core business model, but makes drastic changes that extend well beyond the IT organization. The new digital transformation initiatives lead the organization to debate on whether to continue with the old model or to leverage the innovations provided by the third platform.

For example, the old model had all the important assets behind firewalls while the organization worked with only a few partners. The third platform would enable the hospital to work with a community of potential partners to leverage their core IP. Healthcare organizations could then have the option to enable new business models, such as allowing amplification of values by using cloud services for distributing their products and services. This would also enable partners deliver value-added services by themselves.

Leveraging Cloud Platforms – With mushrooming industry-specific cloud platforms, healthcare industry has the option of leveraging the new generation of third platform solutions that suit its specific industrial needs. New services are coming up that offer levels of value going well beyond the legacy horizontal core business systems such as CRM or ERP. Healthcare industry would do well to take advantage of these new services as early as possible.

Being an Industry-Specific Platform Provider – Hospitals can move beyond merely using industry-specific cloud platforms to becoming industry-specific platform providers. This is a tremendous opportunity to transform their business. For example, hospitals can use the cloud as a place to market and distribute their intellectual property content while using the platform for enabling a community of innovative players who can create, market and distribute their own services.

That allows the hospital to become the center of innovation in the industry while enabling others to distribute content through their portal. This helps the hospital to increase its visibility and viability within the industry.

Using Pre-Integrated Solutions For Industry Digitization – Today, vendors offer a variety of approaches supporting transformation to a digital enterprise. This encompasses the entire field of clouds, mobile, social and analytic solutions including a new generation of finely focused point solutions. These can fast-track the digitization of critical and fast-evolving processes.

Revamping The Intelligent Infrastructure, Customer Analytics and Digital Commerce – By implementing the third platform solutions, the healthcare industry can use a wide variety of initiatives for digital transformation. This includes new ways in which companies reach out to customers, learn about their preferences and behavior, while at the same time, develop innovations.

Finding Suitable Partners – One of the important components of the third platform is that instead of trying to do everything by themselves, healthcare organizations must outsource their non-core activities. That will allow them to focus on their core competence while taking advantage of their partners' expertise in accelerating their journey towards innovation and growth. Partners must be able to provide world-class competence in third platform solutions and have the best practices and acumen for business consulting to help in the transition.

CONCLUSION

Healthcare organizations planning to embark on a journey on the third platform must not shirk from reinventing themselves. Not only will this help them become the IT organization of the third platform, they should also try to become the enterprises of the third platform. The transformation to the third platform has already started and those not considering moving forward now may find the competition is leaving them behind.

REFERENCES

Exploring Enterprise IT Transformation During the Transition to "Third Platform" Technologies

http://enterprise.huawei.com/en/about/e-journal/ict/detail/hw-275497.htm

As IDC Sees It, Tech's 'Third Platform' Disrupts Everyone

http://www.cio.com/article/2377568/cloud-computing/as-idc-sees-it-tech-s-third-platform-disrupts-everyone.html

Future Points to Healthcare IT as a Service

http://www.cio.com/article/2834834/healthcare/future-points-to-healthcare-it-as-a-service.html

The 3rd Platform: Enabling Digital Transformation

http://www.tcs.com/SiteCollectionDocuments/White-Papers/3rd-Platform-Enabling-Digital-Transformation.pdf

YOUR PATIENT'S HEALTH DATA IN THE CLOUDS

New technology is revolutionizing healthcare. Proliferation of laptops, smartphones and tablets can be witnessed in medical institutions, helping doctors to connect in better ways with their patients. Medical workers can connect almost instantaneously to obtain the medical information they seek.

However, risks follow new technologies. For example, a laptop may be easily misplaced or stolen. If that laptop has the personal information of several thousand patients stored on it, its theft may lead to lawsuit settlements reaching up to $100,000. Therefore, hospitals need to be careful about how they are collecting, storing and protecting the information on their patients.

Storing data on mobile devices may make it easier to access, but it also increases the risk of the same data falling into wrong hands if the device is misplaced. It does not matter much if the data on the device was encrypted. Patients (and the law) care more about the actual loss of personal information rather than the loss of the doctor's laptop on which that information resided. Therefore, protecting the data itself is a better proposition for ensuring the safety of patient records. Putting data on secure cloud applications is one way of minimizing risks from theft, provided it cannot be downloaded into any type of computer.

HOW DOES CLOUD STORAGE WORK?

Google Cloud Storage is one simple and practical example of a working cloud storage. This popular online application Google Docs makes preparing, editing, storing and sharing documents online very easy for a user without the need to download anything to his or her computer. If necessary, users do have the option to download as well.

For a hospital, it would be trivial to set up a system that stores all documents in encrypted form on Google Cloud. Doctors and nurses could read and update these documents online in the cloud. With nothing available on the device, criminals will have nothing to gain by stealing tablets or laptops.

Hospital staff could be using thousands of mobile devices. Authorizing all the different makes and encrypting them could be a formidable task for the IT department. With the patients' data safe in the clouds, IT need only secure the network connecting to the cloud to make it impenetrable for outsiders. Additionally, this leaves busy doctors and nurses to focus more for their patients rather than worrying about the security of the data on their computers. Investing in such robust security has another advantage – it is a less expensive proposition in the long run.

HEALTHCARE INFRASTRUCTURE AS A SERVICE

Many cloud service providers offer IaaS or Infrastructure as a Service for the healthcare industry. These are typically, well-managed, highly secure cloud computing platforms optimized for critical healthcare workloads. Hospitals may opt for a bare metal or a virtual server deployment and have complete control over the configuration of the server, the operating system used and applications for storage and deployment.

Such Infrastructure as a Service offers many benefits to the healthcare industry. Hospitals have the option to install dedicated servers and storage. With comprehensive Service-Level Agreements or

SLAs, hospitals are ensured of flexible scaling and the benefits of cloud economics.

With IaaS, the healthcare facility can get a cloud environment of their choice – hybrid, shared or dedicated. Providers offer several advantages such as high availability with real-time monitoring and alerting. Most offer highly redundant system design, ranging from networks to power supplies along with ITIL-compliant security, patching and monitoring.

HOW RELIABLE IS THE CLOUD IT INFRASTRUCTURE

Cloud service providers allow the healthcare facility to focus their internal resources on patient engagement, clinical initiatives and many other services for the improvement of patient outcomes. Hospitals should look for IaaS that is exclusively created for healthcare organizations. Cloud IT infrastructures usually provide support for Operating Systems such as Unix, Linux and Windows, apart from offering advanced big data capabilities along with optimization for analytics.

Hospitals can expect high levels of resiliency, improved memory capacity and advanced levels of processor and storage performance from cloud service providers. Apart from managing the infrastructure, these providers also manage the hypervisor related to the operating system and the application level. They also take care of patch management to keep the system up to date and consistent to the required level of quality.

DOES HIPAA APPROVE OF CLOUD STORAGE?

The emergence of HIPAA-compliant cloud storage has raised the bar of providing a complete solution for improved performance and security for the service providers. The improved access to information stored on HIPAA-compliant cloud simplifies switching and leads to more savings for the medical facilities.

The US Department of Health and Human Services had found physical theft to be the single-most type of large data breach at most healthcare systems. However, such data breaches were virtually non-existent when hospitals stored the information of their patients on HIPAA-compliant cloud systems.

HIPAA-compliant healthcare software meets the government's security standards when storing or transmitting data. Industry preferred encryption products are used to protect customer data while transmitting between the service and the customer's network. As a first line of defense against unwanted access to their systems, most services use a commercial-grade firewall.

Whatever data security is currently in use, the certification is never one-time. This is an ongoing exercise and IT experts must work diligently to stay ahead of potential threats. Most HIPAA-compliant cloud services maintain their data-centers in multiple locations with maximum-security standards. Some even require additional security clearance for physical access to their servers within the data center.

HOW DOES USING A CLOUD SERVICE REDUCE THE RISK OF DATA LOSS?

Cloud service providers that store data securely in multiple places minimize the risk of data loss due to catastrophic natural disasters, sabotage or destruction. Redundancy is assured when the healthcare information is stored on primary database servers along with a backup database server. Providers ensure that customer's data can be replicated to database servers in real-time during disaster recovery operations.

For healthcare services to attain this level of data, security would turn out to be extremely expensive and administratively very difficult. It would detract from the healthcare provider's primary functionality of caring for their patients. However, when a cloud service provider offers security, it is less expensive as the implementation is usually on a large scale. On one hand, the healthcare industry gets security at affordable prices and on the other, it is not burdened with maintaining a service that is not its core strength.

Although the cloud hosts and protects medical information, the control remains with the hospital. With support from the cloud service provider, hospitals can ensure a role-based security system for accessing the data. Users can have different levels of access based on their roles within the hospital's organization. Security breaches become easier to prevent, as specific people now require different levels of security clearance. The hospital can choose to employ role-based security for preventing an employee from unwittingly altering or accessing information that he or she is not permitted to because of their specific function.

From their side, cloud service providers offer a host of security features that their customers can utilize. For ensuring compliance to HIPAA, there are password complexity requirements, verification questions and session lockouts. Providers typically store user passwords with one-way hashing algorithms, while logging user entries with date, time and source IP address. The logs are maintained for a minimum of 30 days to ensure tracking and security.

THINGS TO CONSIDER WHEN SELECTING A CLOUD SERVICE PROVIDER

As with any technology, there are risks involved with cloud services as well. Being a new environment, hospitals need to be vigilant and understand the risks they will face if their data is breached.

Cloud infrastructure tends to distribute their operating expenses with multi-tenancy, while providing decoupling between hardware resources and applications by working with several third parties. Hospitals need to gain information about who is potentially accessing their data.

One very important measure of security that hospitals should ask to see is the service provider's reliability reports – how much downtime the service provider experiences. The downtime should meet the requirements of the hospital's business. Hospitals must also find out if the cloud service provider is employing exception monitoring systems.

Hospitals that deal with highly sensitive data, for example, information related to HIV treatments, should find out about the hosting company that the provider utilizes. Additionally, they should also seek an independent audit of the security status employed.

Apart from HIPAA, there are not many stringent standards that the nascent cloud industry has to currently follow. However, cloud service providers should know about ISO27001, which deals with third party audit and preferably implement OECD principles that govern the security of information and network systems. Some cloud service providers also follow the SAS70 auditing standard.

Users of cloud services may not know where their information is being held. This brings up the question of jurisdiction, where data might be considered secure in one country but may not be secure in another. It would be prudent for the hospital to ensure beforehand that they are legally assured of the security of their data at all times.

PRELIMINARY CHECKLIST WHEN PLANNING FOR CLOUD SERVICES

- Are exception monitoring systems in place?

- Can staff inadvertently gain access privileges they are not allowed?

- Where will the data be stored, and what data protection laws are prevalent there?

- Which third parties are involved with the provider and if they can access your data?

- Is it possible to have an independent security audit of the host?
- Have good policies been developed for creating, protecting and changing passwords?
- Are there any availability guarantees and penalties defined?
- Is it possible to accommodate your own security policies?
- Are any auditing standards followed?

REFERENCES

Healthcare Solutions
http://www.cleardata.com/solutions/

Infographic: Keep your patient health info secure in the cloud
http://blog.gogrid.com/2014/01/22/infographic-keep-your-patient-health-info-secure-in-the-cloud/

HIPAA-Compliant Cloud Storage
http://www.carecloud.com/hipaa-compliant-cloud-storage/

Top five cloud computing security issues
http://www.computerweekly.com/news/2240089111/Top-five-cloud-computing-security-issues

THE PRESSURE ON HOSPITALS TO IMPROVE THE QUALITY OF MEASUREMENT, PAYMENT AND BILLING SYSTEMS

The Quality Improvement activities of hospitals are constantly under threat from escalating demands of patients and stakeholders. Identification of weaknesses leads to the financial and reputational interests of hospitals coming under increasing pressures to demonstrate higher quality. For example, insurers or payers require hospitals to be accredited for reimbursement. According to the Joint Commission, hospitals seeking accreditation must demonstrate compliance with the National Patient Safety Goals, which are a set of standards addressing patient safety issues such as reduction of hospital-acquired infections and more.

The Annual Payment Update program of the CMS or Centers for Medicare and Medicaid Services collects data from hospitals regarding a core set of quality measures. Not participating in the program or failing to meet the reporting requirements of CMS means that the hospital's annual payment update receives a two-percentage-point reduction. Lately, CMS has escalated this to disallowing payments to hospitals over 'never events'. These relate to medical errors such as preventable post-operative deaths and foreign bodies left in post-surgery patients.

Hospitals try countless incremental fixes such as implementing electronic medical records, turning patients into better consumers, enforcing practice guidelines, reducing errors and attacking fraud. Despite most health care systems having excellent leaders and policy makers, well-trained clinicians and well-intentioned physicians, hospitals are beset with uneven quality and rising costs. Therefore, it is time the healthcare system tries out a completely new strategy.

MAXIMIZING THE VALUE FOR PATIENTS

Currently, healthcare systems are supply-driven, with activities organized around what the physicians do. The focus is around the activities of the physicians and geared towards the volume and profitability of services provided – clinical tests, procedures, hospitalizations and physician visits. This is actually a fragmented system wherein every provider offers a full range of services, with the least concentration on what is best for the patient.

Maximizing the value for patients means achieving best outcomes for patients at the lowest costs. The healthcare system requires changing over to a patient-centric system revolving round the needs of the patient. Healthcare must offer services for specific medical conditions that are concentrated in organizations of health-delivery and in the right locations for delivering high-value care.

Most hospitals pay salaries to their nurses – considered a necessary cost of doing business. Typically, nurses represent about 35-40% of the direct-care budget of hospitals. In contrast, healthcare systems treat physicians as revenue generators. Accordingly, hospitals charge payers and the CMS for the costs of the resources used for producing the medical care ordered or provided by the physicians. As yet, Medicare payment policies do not have any mechanism for measuring the specific economic contribution of nurses to their hospitals.

A rule, known as the CMS-1533-FC.6, offers the mechanism for doing so. It allows recognition for nursing care that prevents costly complications, preventing hospitals from losing money. Therefore, the Medicare rule clearly demonstrates the potential for nurses' economic value to hospitals.

However, such transformations will not happen in a single step, but requires an all-comprehensive strategy geared towards value agenda. Healthcare delivery requires to be restructured with introduction of metrics for organization, measurements and reimbursements.

While some organizations are at pilot stages exploring the initiatives in individual practice areas, others have implemented large-scale changes introducing multiple components of the value agenda. The latter are experiencing spectacular improvements in their outcomes and efficiency along with a growing market share.

With well-entrenched interests and practices spanning several decades, hospitals may underestimate the challenges of becoming value-based organizations. That means some organizations will lead the way and others will ultimately follow the path of increasing the value of care. However, this transformation must come from within the organization.

Improving value requires several interdependent set of steps that can only come from physicians and provider organizations, especially as the practice of medicine ultimately defines value. However, this also requires all stakeholders in the healthcare system to play their roles. Suppliers, employers, health plans and even patients must contribute their bit in hastening the transformation – finally leading to enhanced benefits for all.

DEFINING HEALTHCARE GOALS

The first step healthcare organizations must take to solve their problem is to define the proper goal. Pursuit of wrong goals or lack of clarity about the goal will certainly hobble all efforts to reform health care. Distractions such as boosting profits, containing costs and improving access to care are narrow goals and must be avoided. The objective is not to reduce cost at the expense of quality or provide access to poor quality of care. Organizations must realize that profits depend not on delivering good results, but rather on increasing the volume of services aligned with the interests of patients.

Care providers and other stakeholders should be aiming for an all-comprehensive goal of improving value for patients. They should define value as health outcomes important to patients, relative to the cost of attaining those outcomes. Improving the value then comes from either improving one or more outcomes without increasing costs or lowering costs without sacrificing outcomes, or both. Failure to improve value leads to disaster.

Moving towards the value agenda demands a complete departure from the past methods of operation. Essentially, the senior management and board level must commit to the goal of value. Although healthcare organizations prefer to improve outcomes, they focus more on maintaining margins and growing volumes. Therefore, even with noble mission statements, hospitals bypass the actual work of improving value. For decades, hospitals have been following legacy payment structures and delivery approaches. This has set up a vicious circle of reinforcing problems while producing a system that cannot sustain costs and offers erratic quality.

With severe pressures on costs and payers aggressively favoring performance-based reimbursements, hospitals are finally moving away from the fee-for-service arrangements. Moreover, the US Medicare and Medicaid is covering an increasing number of patients, reimbursing them for a fraction of private-plan levels. Therefore, more physicians are opting out of private practice, preferring rather to become salaried employees of hospitals, which in turn are joining health systems in increasing numbers.

THE VALUE TRANSFORMATION STRATEGY

Although external stakeholders regularly impose narrow solutions, these typically preserve existing roles within the healthcare system, not attacking the root cause of the problem. Hospitals must have a strategic agenda that allows them to move to high-value healthcare delivery systems. Such agenda typically has six components that are interdependent and reinforce each other mutually. Health care systems see the greatest progress if these multiple components advance together.

Generate IPUs or Integrated Practice Units: The hospital must give topmost priority to organize its activities around the patient and their need. Therefore, there must be a shift from the siloed organization present today such as specialty departments and provision of discrete services to being organized around the medical condition of the patient. IPUs typically make up a dedicated team containing both clinical and non-clinical personnel to provide a complete care cycle based on the condition of the patient.

Track Outcomes and Costs for Each Patient: Following familiar principles in management, measuring results produces the fastest improvements in any field. Teams strive to improve and excel by pursuing the advancement over time and contrasting their performance to that of peers both within and external to the organization. This metric is independent of country and a very crucial step in improving health care – results improve with systematic measurement of value such as for outcome and costs.

Use Care Cycles with Bundled Payments: Currently, value of care does not directly improve by the dominant payment models such as fee-for-service or global capitation. A single payment covering all leads to providers spending less, but there is no incentive for improving outcome or value. A better approach is a bundled payment covering a care cycle. For acute medical conditions, this can cover the full care cycle, whereas for chronic conditions, this can be for a defined period. Provided these are well-designed, bundled payment can directly encourage teamwork and lead to high-value care.

Generate Integrated Care Delivery Systems: Most healthcare delivery organizations are typically spread out over multiple sites. Such stand-alone sites are not exactly true delivery systems, but loose confederations that often provide duplicate services. With integrated care delivery systems, providers have a huge opportunity to improve value by eliminating duplication and fragmentation of care. Additionally, this optimizes the types of care that hospitals deliver at each location.

Extend the Geographic Reach: Most academic medical centers and healthcare delivery systems serve only their immediate geographic locations. For large scale, substantial increase of value, specialty hospitals catering to specific medical conditions must reach out to more patients. They can do this by extending their reach by strategically expanding their excellent IPUs. However, this should not mean buying full-service practices or hospitals in new areas – the focus must be on improving value and not on simply augmenting volume.

Generate Supporting Information Technology Platforms: This sixth component of the value agenda provides a stable and fundamental support to the preceding five. Typically, in healthcare, IT systems are siloed by type of data, type of service, location and department. Very often, IT systems tend to obscure rather than reinforce integrated, multidisciplinary care. However, with the right type of IT system, IPUs can work efficiently with one another, allow measurement and provide methodology for new reimbursements. Parts of a properly designed delivery system work cohesively with a proper IT support platform.

CONCLUSION

The market does not retain reputations based on perception. Providers that insist on following the broken system will gradually find themselves antiquated. Regardless of whether they are small or big, communities or academic, organizations that adopt the value agenda will find not only financial viability, but also reputation based on excellence in outcomes and will take pride in the value they can deliver.

REFERENCES

New Medicare Payment Rules: Danger or Opportunity for Nursing?
http://www.nursingcenter.com/lnc/journalarticle?Article_ID=798117

The Strategy That Will Fix Health Care
https://hbr.org/2013/10/the-strategy-that-will-fix-health-care/

Hospital Strategies to Engage Physicians in Quality Improvement
http://www.hschange.com/CONTENT/1087/

PRIVACY AND SECURITY OF HEALTH INFORMATION

The Health Information Management profession has prided itself over ensuring the confidentiality, security and privacy of personal health information as a fundamental principle, throughout its long history. Today, as electronic systems increasingly distribute information, HIM professionals continue to face the challenges of maintaining the security and privacy of patient information, with their efforts getting more complex every day. The constantly changing regulatory and legislative environment also adds to this challenge of responsibility.

According to the Privacy Rule, overall confidentiality of protected health information is to be maintained regardless of type – electronic, paper or verbal. The Security Rule applies only for protected health information in electronic form. The Final HITECH Omnibus Rule is applicable for strengthening the overall privacy and security protections.

As has been witnessed in medical practice, patients are more likely to share sensitive information only if they trust their confidentiality will be honored. That makes trust extremely important clinically and a key business asset for the healthcare industry. HIM professionals can cultivate the trust of their patients by:

- Making sure patients can access their own medical records
- Handling health information such that privacy of the patient remains protected
- Maintaining accurate records of individual patients.
- Why is Privacy and Security Necessary?

One of the core requirements of the Medicare and Medicaid Electronic Health Record Programs is that privacy and security of patient health information be protected. Furthermore, effective privacy and security measures protect clinical practices from civil and criminal penalties. Some examples of privacy and security measures that clinical practices have are private examination rooms, a notice of privacy practices, and secure ways of transmitting patient information for billing.

Realization of potential benefits from exchange of electronic health information comes from maintaining information as EHRs or electronic health records and by ensuring the privacy and security of the health information. Sometimes, participants or individuals in a network may not trust the electronic exchange of information because of the lack of accuracy and completeness of such information or because of perceived or actual risks to EHI. Such cases may lead to life-threatening consequences, as they may not be willing to disclose necessary health information.

Protecting the confidentiality, integrity and availability of health information in the EHR is entirely the responsibility of the healthcare practice and not of the EHR vendor. Likewise, complying with the Meaningful Use requirements of CMS and the Privacy and Security Rules of HIPAA are also the responsibility of the healthcare practice alone.

REQUIREMENTS OF MEANINGFUL USE

HIPAA privacy and security requirements embedded in the EHR Incentive Programs insist on meaningful use requirements. There are two stages of Meaningful Use –

Stage 1: Objective #12 – Patients are to be provided with an electronic copy of their health information upon request. This includes diagnostic test results, problems list, medication list, medication allergies.

Stage 1: Objective #15 – Implement appropriate technical capabilities and certified EHR technology to protect electronic health records created or maintained.

Stage 2: Core and Menu Objectives – Providers must comply with a core and menu structure of a predetermined number of menu objectives for demonstrating meaningful use.

All providers must demonstrate their compliance to stage 1 of Meaningful Use, before they are eligible to move to Stage 2. Eligible professionals, hospitals and critical access hospitals must meet specific criteria to participate in Stage 2 of the Medicare and Medicaid EHR Incentive Programs.

Under Objective #12 of Stage 1 MU, the Privacy Rule of HIPAA states that patients have the right to view and obtain a copy of their PHI, including their information stored in the EHR. The metric for this objective is the number of patients who receive an electronic copy of their requested PHI within three business days and this should be more than 50% of total requests made.

Under Objective #15 of Stage 1 MU, the Security Rule of HIPAA states that healthcare entities must implement policies and procedures to prevent, detect, contain and correct security violations. The metric for this objective is the review of a security risk analysis conducted and the security updates implemented as necessary. Additionally, identified security deficiencies must be corrected as part of the risk management process.

COMPLYING WITH THE MU PRIVACY REQUIREMENTS

When a hospital or a medical professional adopts an EHR, they should take time to identify any gaps in how their practice fulfills its responsibilities for applicable laws such as the HIPAA Privacy Rule. For meeting Meaningful Use requirements, they must focus on privacy to compliment the security risk analysis process in a four-step process –

1. Know the HIPAA Privacy Rule: Update the knowledge of HIPAA Privacy Rule requirements. For example, the Notice of Privacy Practices must inform patients of their privacy rights to the health information.

2. Review State Privacy Laws: Several professional associations or state agencies analyze the interaction between the HIPAA Privacy Rules and the state privacy law. Such analysis is referred to as a HIPAA preemption analysis. Professionals must contact their associations and refer to such available analysis for the specific state.

3. Review the adherence of the practice to Federal and State Privacy Requirements: Consider changes that will allow the medical practice conform to nationally accepted principles and state laws regarding patient privacy. Be aware that privacy and security requirements could change with release of new rules.

4. Foresee and forestall Patient Privacy concerns: When digitizing health information, the hospital or the professional should address any privacy concerns the patients may have. As an integral part of the overall patient engagement strategy, patients may need reassurance that the EHR will actually safeguard their privacy.

COMPLYING WITH MU SECURITY REQUIREMENTS

As part of the high-level security risk analysis process, the focus should be on the core measures of meaningful use. Therefore, the risks necessary to be analyzed and maintained will refer to:

- Security vulnerabilities such as improper configuration of user access controls or staff able to view PHI inappropriately.

- Threats to PHI such as theft or loss of portable devices that store or access patient information.

This means the hospital or HMI professional should perform a security review of the electronic health care system to correct any practice that could make the patients' PHI vulnerable. Such security updates could be software upgrades, changes in storage methods or work flow processes, new or updated procedures and policies, staff training or any other corrective action necessary to eliminate the security deficiency or deficiencies that the risk analysis has identified.

IDENTIFYING RISKS TO MEDICAL PRACTICES

Patient information requires two phases of protection – initiation and maintenance. Before initiating a set of safeguards, hospitals require conducting a security risk analysis for identifying and prioritizing risks to formulate a risk mitigation strategy and to apply it. Later, maintaining the risk management strategy requires the hospitals to conduct an ongoing cyclical process of reviewing the current security measures, identifying new risks, re-assessing risks identified earlier, planning ways to mitigate risks identified and monitoring and evaluating the results.

HOW IS A SECURITY RISK ANALYSIS CONDUCTED?

Doctors examine and test a patient to assess clinical risks and to diagnose a condition. Then they use the diagnosis and other clinical data to plan treatment. In a similar way, a security risk analysis examines and assesses perceived and actual risks of a breach and diagnoses the reasons for the breach. This diagnosis is used to create an action plan that will make the practice better at protecting patient information. Just as chronic diseases require treatment, privacy and security require continuous monitoring and evaluation, with periodic adjustments.

Conducting a security risk involves systematic and continuous processes of -

- Examining and identifying potential threats and vulnerabilities when protecting information in medical practices.
- Implementing changes for making PHI more secure than at present
- Monitoring results (risk management)

According to the HIPAA Security Rule, all covered entities must conduct a risk analysis for identifying risks and vulnerabilities to their electronic PHI. With risk analysis, an organization takes the first step towards its efforts of compliance with the Security Rule. Health care practices can follow HIPAA risk analysis guidelines to help establish and implement necessary safeguards based on the unique circumstances of their practice.

Health care practices must employ risk analysis as an ongoing process to gain a detailed understanding of the confidentiality, integrity and availability of e-PHI. Providers must employ risk analysis to address such criteria by evaluating the impact of and the likelihood of potential breaches. Based on this analysis, they must implement security features, catalog them and maintain the security protections.

A covered health care provider retains the ultimate responsibility for HIPAA compliance. That includes the security risk analysis as well. For completing the risk analysis, covered entities have several options, including doing it in-house, hiring an outside professional, or enlisting the assistance of REC staff. Whatever be the method used, security analysis will require a direct involvement of the management of the covered entity.

CONCLUSION

Good patient care comes from safe record-keeping practices. EHRs represent a valuable and unique human being and not just a collection of data to be guarded. By adopting an EHR and sharing the patient health information electronically, healthcare institutes open up new risks for which they need newer ways of securing information. The healthcare industry requires sustained efforts to update privacy and security practices to make them manageable and affordable.

REFERENCES

Health Information Privacy, Security, and Your EHR
http://www.healthit.gov/providers-professionals/ehr-privacy-security

Privacy & Security
http://www.ahima.org/topics/psc

Guide to Privacy and Security of Health Information
http://www.healthit.gov/sites/default/files/pdf/privacy/privacy-and-security-guide.pdf

Stage 2
http://www.cms.gov/Regulations-and-Guidance/Legislation/EHRIncentivePrograms/Stage_2.html

Made in the USA
Middletown, DE
13 July 2016